The Information Management Engine™
A Profit Prescription for the Business Ultimatum™

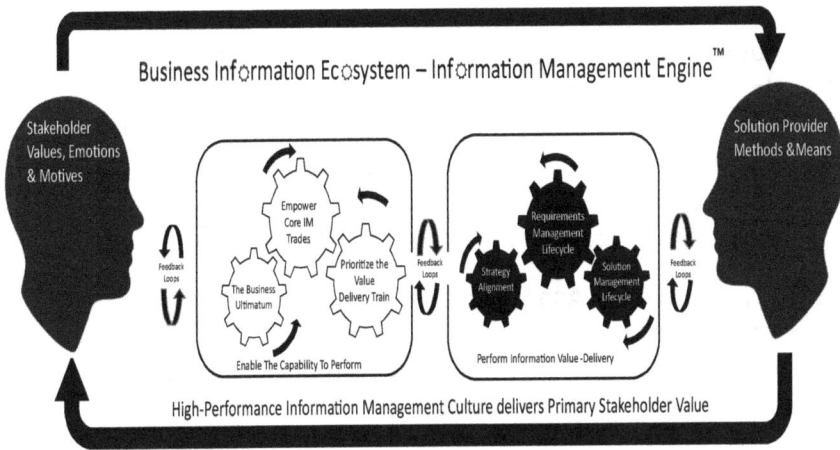

Business Information Ecosystem – Information Management Engine™

Stakeholder Values, Emotions & Motives

Solution Provider Methods & Means

Empower Core IM Trades

Prioritize the Value Delivery Train

The Business Ultimatum

Feedback Loops

Requirements Management Lifecycle

Strategy Alignment

Solution Management Lifecycle

Feedback Loops

Enable The Capability To Perform

Perform Information Value -Delivery

High-Performance Information Management Culture delivers Primary Stakeholder Value

By

Gerrold Kimbrough CBAP®, PMP®, ITIL®

Business Analysis ◆ Project Management ◆ IT Service Management

Cover Design: Michael Trent
Editors: Gerrold Kimbrough, Corinne Colbert

DEDICATION

To the fondest memories of my loving mom, Maxine Kimbrough, who demonstrated daily the importance of hard work, education, persistence, and perseverance.

ACKNOWLEDGMENTS

All peace and glory to the Living God; in humble prayer, I give you all thanks.

Special thanks to my wonderful wife and children for your love, patience, and support. I am forever grateful.

Thanks to all my closest family and friends (you know who you are) for your love, care, and support.

Thanks to all my career mentors, co-workers, teammates, and friends who have patiently endured my many faults, imperfections, and mistakes. I am so thankful to you and wish you much success in all your endeavors.

Table of Contents

Lists of Tables

Table of Figures

Introduction

The Nature of Information for Survival and Growth

Survival and growth are two of the most primal passions driving the necessity for accurate, timely, and relevant information. Instinctive reactions to environmental information often determine a natural organism's survival or extinction. For example, when zebras can't see lions hiding in tall grass on the African savannah, the zebras become food for the lions. On the other hand, if lions don't naturally realize that zebras prefer to eat grass and live in large herds, they won't evolve the camouflage and hunting strategies required to catch zebras. Indeed, it does not take much observation to realize that information is a basic survival requirement for all living organisms and the organizations they may form. This reality includes human beings.

Each of our five senses detect, receive, and send information to our brains to process and react within environments and situations: fight or flight, sink or swim, do or don't responses, for example. Our sensory organs (eyes, ears, nose, mouth, and skin) are apparently *designed* to process the relevant information needed to survive, thrive, and grow. I strongly suggest reading Diane Ackerman's book, "A Natural History of the Senses." It provides a wonderful exploration of how our senses work, their role in nature, and the fascinating reasons behind them. Information has played a crucial role in the lives of living beings for countless years in the past, and it will continue to do so in the future. Just like water is essential for rain and sunlight for a sunrise, the need for information is fundamental to life and organization. These two elements go hand in hand, and you cannot have one without the other.

The significance of information for survival and progress is obvious. We can see its impact in various aspects of life, from plants and animals to human achievements and organizations. Consider, for instance, how a beautiful houseplant knows exactly when and how to orient its leaves towards the sun for optimal growth. Or think about how reindeer instinctively choose the right paths during their long migrations spanning hundreds of miles. Additionally, think about the motivations and passions that drove innovators like Jeff Bezos, the founder of Amazon, to create a more efficient distribution system for music and books. These examples highlight how information influences the natural world and drives human success and accomplishments.

Abraham Maslow, a well-known psychologist, proposed a theory (1943, 1954) that suggests human behavior is driven by the satisfaction of five levels of needs. These needs encompass fundamental physical requirements such as food, water, warmth, rest, as well as safety needs related to health and security. Now, consider the crucial role of timely, accurate, and reliable information in meeting these basic needs. How do we determine which paths to take, what decisions to make, or what to avoid when seeking food, clothing, and shelter? Is it through traditional knowledge passed down through generations, observing others, or recognizing signs of success? Information plays a vital role at every level.

In reality, information could be considered a vital human need alongside the ones identified by Maslow. It is crucial for the survival and development of all living beings. The need for information, driven by our instinct for survival, can account for the evolutionary advancements and technological innovations we observe. For instance, the natural senses of various organisms, like bats using radar or dogs with their keen hearing, showcase how information acquisition contributes to their adaptation and survival. Furthermore, breakthroughs in information technology, such as artificial intelligence, robotic process automation, and the Internet of Things, demonstrate our ongoing efforts to harness and leverage information for progress and improvement.

The Role of Information in Business Survival

According to the Merriam-Webster dictionary, information is described as knowledge acquired through investigation, study, or instruction. It involves being aware of facts, data, or intelligence related to a specific person, place, or thing. Personally, I strongly believe that information plays a crucial role in the lives of living beings. This belief is supported by the fact that natural instincts represent a form of built-in information-to-action-reaction connections, ranging from instinctive responses to future-oriented foresight, depending on the perspective we consider.

In addition to the simple definition of information, let's also consider the perspective of Claude Shannon, a brilliant mathematician often referred to as "the father of information theory." According to Shannon, information can be seen as the means to resolve uncertainty. In practical terms, when we have accurate and relevant information at our disposal, it helps us reduce uncertainty and make more informed decisions. This, in turn, fuels our desire for even better information, as we understand its value in guiding our actions effectively. This idea of reducing uncertainty is equally vital for organizations, as they strive to identify and measure the key factors that contribute to their success. It is often said that "what gets measured, gets done," underscoring the importance of measuring and tracking the right elements to achieve desired outcomes.

Too often, IT professionals have focused on the "T" in information technology, unintentionally losing sight of the critical nature of the "I" in every aspect of the operation—especially when the information in question pertains to primary stakeholders' personal values and emotional motivations.

For instance, consider those who give a project their all due to burning desires to realize a dream, ambition, or heartfelt aspiration. Think about the critical thirst for insight and understanding behind Thomas Edison's many inventions. What role did information quality play in the many cycles of experimentation? As a result of that process, we now enjoy the many benefits of electric-powered light bulbs and many other inventions.

In any economic situation, business owners and investors have a common goal: to make sure that

Introduction

their investments result in predictable returns for investors and provide customers with valuable experiences. They aim to achieve this by increasing returns, improving profit margins, reducing operating costs, and enhancing customer experiences. These factors are the driving forces behind commercial investments, as they contribute to the overall success and sustainability of businesses.

Given the preeminence of information in every aspect of our lives and organizations—and the fact that we are inundated with large volumes of information, or Big Data—it's equally important to acknowledge the imperative to manage the *information technologies* we use to reap the benefits of valuable information. These include computers, smart phones, microchips, telecommunications equipment, and related technologies.

Therefore, the main purpose of this book is to assist organizations in delivering value to their stakeholders by incorporating effective information technology practices, alongside other essential business management disciplines. At the heart of thriving information ecosystems within organizations lies what I refer to as the **Information Management Engine**™. This book specifically aims to empower business owners, leaders, computer users, and knowledge workers to harness the full potential of their organization's data. It provides insights and strategies to tackle the various challenges posed by the **Business Ultimatum**™. This term represents the combination of *economic obstacles, emotional hurdles, legal* and *regulatory* requirements, *competitive pressures, internal barriers and*

The Information Management Engine

constraints that organizations encounter on their
path towards fulfilling stakeholders' emotional
goals and achieving value realization.

To this end, it's essential to make clear that
the drive for better information is necessary to
actionable intelligence concerning which internal
factors (e.g., emotion, energy, motive) and
external influences (e.g., competitive,
environmental, etc.) are relevant for a person,
team, or organization to prioritize.

It's tempting to think that the need for data
quality and information integrity management is so
obvious that we need not spend much time
discussing it. After all, it's common sense,
correct? Everyone knows the axiom of garbage in-
garbage out. However, it's equally true that "what
is common knowledge may not be common practice."

In his widely acclaimed book, "*The Seven Basic
Habits of Highly Effective People,*" Stephen Covey
explored the essential elements that lead to
success for influential individuals. Drawing from
Covey's insights, I firmly believe that we can
identify a comparable set of habits or factors in
highly effective organizations, particularly in
the business realm. These organizations exhibit
certain patterns and practices in how they
leverage computing systems and processes to drive
their success.

In fact, it is widely recognized that effective
businesses understand the importance of leveraging
their information assets to create value for their
customers, stakeholders, and employees. By
utilizing valuable information strategically,
businesses can gain a competitive advantage in the
market. They can enhance customer experiences,
develop innovative products or services, optimize

operational efficiency, and make informed decisions based on data-driven insights. Numerous case studies and success stories exist of companies that have effectively utilized their information assets to achieve sustained growth and market leadership. Examples include technology giants like Google, Microsoft and Amazon, which have built their success on leveraging information effectively.

These successful companies have one important thing in common: they understand the value of their data and know how to use it to achieve business success. Let's take the example of a large consumer goods company in the 1980s. They realized that inaccurate data was causing problems in their decision-making systems, leading to significant financial losses in manufacturing efficiency. To address this issue, they embarked on a project to implement barcodes on all their products and materials. The introduction of barcodes proved to be a game-changer. It enabled them to track their products more effectively, control inventory levels, and improve materials requirements planning. By eliminating manual data entry, factory workers were able to process more items with fewer errors. This improvement in data accuracy had a ripple effect throughout the company, leading to further enhancements in their operations.

Similar projects occurred in the retail sector to improve data accuracy at point-of-sale. Younger readers may not realize that grocery prices were not always swiped into the cash register. Instead, retailers had to hire cashiers proficient at entering accurate data quickly to keep pace with long lines of customers.

The Information Management Engine

As good as many of these employees were, the error rates ultimately cost employers millions of dollars. Inaccurate data results in poor order and restocking decisions, which leads to higher inventory costs and other results that do not make investors or business owners very happy. It is easy to take point-of-sale and other similar technology innovations for granted today because we are years past their groundbreaking, innovative introductions. Many are second nature to newer generations of business owners and customers.

From my personal experiences and extensive reading, I strongly believe that the advantages of working with data go beyond technological improvements alone. The attitudes, work habits, and beliefs of employees who handle data also play a significant role in reflecting its importance. These employees understand their responsibilities in maintaining data entry integrity and ensuring quality assurance. They recognize the value of accurate and reliable data and actively contribute to upholding its integrity. Their commitment and dedication contribute to the overall success and effectiveness of data-driven processes within an organization.

In most companies, crucial personnel are entrusted with the important task of capturing or facilitating data entry into computer systems. This responsibility falls upon various roles such as call center operators, sales order entry clerks, warehouse purchasing and receivables clerks, materials handlers, delivery drivers, nurse assistants, office assistants, paralegals, secretaries, engineers, and line workers. It is their collective effort that ensures the proper functioning of these systems, which greatly

Introduction

impacts the overall well-being and success of their organization, whether it be a business, church, or school.

When employees utilize available technology to enhance the speed, accuracy, and consistency of data entry, it brings significant advantages to the business. Technologies such as robotic process automation, machine learning, and artificial intelligence offer even greater efficiencies and innovative solutions. In Part III, we will delve into the role of data stewards and key personas who play a critical part in the success of data-driven organizations. It is important to recognize their essential contribution to achieving organizational success through effective data management!

PART I: Enable Information Value-Delivery Performance

Similar to any asset, the value of information depends on various factors within an organization. These factors include the current environment, market position, intellectual capital, workforce motivations, research and development efforts, and other important considerations. Just like anticipating future value, the potential value of an asset, such as information, needs to be carefully calculated, assessed, monitored, and effectively managed. This is crucial for those responsible for delivering it and for those who expect to benefit from it.

Certain key entities in our society play a vital role in transforming crucial data and information assets into tangible value. These entities include schools, organizations, and companies. Their responsibility is to unlock the potential value within data and information, making it evident and measurable. This value exchange is essential for individuals such as students, employees, customers, or investors who have certain expectations regarding the value they receive in return for their involvement or investment.

The main accountability of those responsible for delivering value is to ensure, without a doubt, that they have the necessary resources and capabilities to drive task performance. This is crucial to achieve desired outcomes consistently. They need to make sure that these resources are available, scalable, sustainable, and well-maintained over time. The initial step in achieving this goal is to recognize that nothing less than this level of commitment is sufficient to address the ultimate challenge: the choice between survival and growth or the risk of disappearing altogether.

Embrace the Business Ultimatum
with
*Applied Management Science, Certified-Professional
Trade Practice, and Emotional Intelligence*

Business information ecosystems—consisting of
content, information technologies, business
processes, and training—are powerful tools in the
hands of expert, motivated professionals guided by
inspirational leadership. These systems drive pivotal
cause and effect, such as technology platforms to
research and act on urgent business questions and
critical success factors that lead to crucial
customer insight and investor returns. The first of
these success factors is an organization with a
healthy understanding of the business ultimatum that
pervades and motivates for-profit organizations.

The Business Ultimatum, as I define it, encompasses
all the challenges that organizations face in
achieving stakeholder satisfaction. These challenges
include emotional hurdles, economic obstacles, legal
and regulatory requirements, competitive pressures,
internal barriers, and financial obstacles that
impact stakeholders' emotional, physical, and
financial well-being. In simple terms, the Business
Ultimatum sets a clear directive for commercial
enterprises: it's a decisive call to action,
requiring them to succeed or fail, adapt or perish,
act promptly or miss out, and make a profit or incur
a loss. Specifically, the Business Ultimatum is an
undeniable edict for all commercial endeavors.

This ultimatum is at the heart of all the plans,
goals, objectives, dreams, and ambitions of anyone
starting a for-profit company. Regardless of the

entrepreneur's original motive, it remains a dream deferred until the enterprise generates a sustainable profit and *hurdle rate*.[1]

The Business Ultimatum is inferred from statements like *do or die, sink or swim, fly or fall,* and *now or never.* One of my favorites is *win-win or no deal.* In *The Seven Basic Habits of Highly Effective People,* Stephen Covey describes *win-win* as a character ethic that advocates mutually beneficial relationships as a keystone of a healthy business environment.

Some may argue that "Win-Win" is not an actual ultimatum, but rather a guiding principle that aligns with the ideal mindset for the Business Ultimatum. This perspective emphasizes the significance of finding a balance that serves the collective interests of all parties involved. It recognizes the importance of satisfying customers, investors, and employees, as well as delivering value both internally and externally. By adopting a Win-Win approach, organizations can strive for mutual benefits and sustainable success.

When employees believe that their employers genuinely value them, they tend to be more motivated to work harder and smarter to get the job done. Recognizing employees' need to have control over their work and work environment contributes to their productivity.[2] Savvy business owners and stakeholders strive to create a climate that encourages employees to participate, learn, and share in their workplace's growth and profitability.

---

[1] The minimum return rate from an investment that will offset its total costs. The formula is the Weighted Average Cost of Capital (WACC) + Risk premium

[2] Wiles, J. (2018). "Employees Seek Personal Value and Purpose at Work. Be Prepared to Deliver." Gartner. Retrieved from https://www.gartner.com/smarterwithgartner/employees-seek-personal-value-and-purpose-at-work-be-prepared-to-deliver/

The Information Management Engine

In addition, managers and leaders should seek to inspire employees to feel a personal connection, a sense of pride and accomplishment with their employer. Employers who consistently share important business information and insight with employees help engender buy-in to the employer's Business Ultimatum. "One of the key elements in developing personal identification with the company is an understanding of how the business works."[3]

A concrete path to meeting the challenge of the Business Ultimatum is to apply management sciences, certified-professional trade practices, and emotional intelligence. These are how dreams become action, results, and stakeholder satisfaction.

Embrace Applied Management Science. As we learned in grade school, the scientific method is a logical sequence of steps:

1. Observations or questions
2. Research and hypothesis
3. Experimentation
4. Results and data analysis
5. Conclusion

The essence of management involves planning, organizing, commanding, coordinating, and controlling three primary constraints—budget, schedule, and resources (particularly people, processes, and technology)—to deliver an expected outcome to customers, investors, and organizations. This process applies to all kinds of management: project management, research management, process management, data security management, master data management, inventory management, financial management, sports management, and many others.

Applied management science is a research-based,

---

[3] Kaydos, W. (1991). *Measuring, Managing, and Maximizing Performance*

data-driven, results-oriented approach to decision-making, problem-solving, and opportunity exploitation, using scientific methods to build sustainable, scalable capabilities that demonstrate quantifiable benefits and value. It is a multidisciplinary approach with many practical applications, including air traffic safety and control, financial forecast planning accuracy, railcar scheduling optimization, product distribution and inventory controls, buy-versus-build software decisions—even how to land and operate a rover on Mars. Key practitioners include data scientists, statistical analysts, industrial, and mechanical engineers, aerospace designers, supply chain managers, senior business analysts, large-scale construction project managers, logistics planners, and many more.

One of the tasks that empowers employees with clear capabilities is accurately determining the appropriate budget, technologies, training, partnerships, and support from upper management required to perform effectively in critical moments and beyond. Thankfully, there are reputable organizations and publications dedicated to exploring this topic in-depth, providing valuable resources for further research. We will delve deeper into these resources in subsequent chapters, allowing for a more comprehensive understanding of the subject.

One of the tasks that greatly empowers employees is accurately determining the necessary budget, technologies, training, partnerships, and support from upper management needed to excel in crucial moments and beyond. The good news is that there are outstanding organizations and publications dedicated to exploring this very topic, providing valuable

resources for further research. This includes new
technologies such as Artificial Intelligence (AI),
Machine Learning (ML), Natural Language Processing
(NLP), and Robotic Process Automation (RPA), as well
as training and certification, apprenticeship,
mentoring, and coaching in their fields' specific
core professional trade-practices. In this way,
organizations build capacity and ensure employees'
abilities to perform. In the upcoming chapters, we
will dive deeper into these resources, allowing for a
more comprehensive understanding of the subject.

Embrace Certified-Professional Trade Practices.
It's disheartening to come across work environments
where managers assign tasks without providing
sufficient leadership support for evidence-based,
data-driven, research-supported, and scientific
problem-solving and decision-making methods.
Achieving a balance between meeting the demands of
the Business Ultimatum and fulfilling the supply side
requires the use of proven methods and appropriate
tools. These enable trade professionals to address
crucial questions that uncover the root causes of
problems and consistently deliver measurable value.

Certified-Professional Trade Practices play a vital
role in effectively managing the challenges of the
Business Ultimatum. Consider the importance of best
practice standards in ensuring health and safety
procedures in hospitals or safely operating a space
station, constructing towering skyscrapers, or
building magnificent suspension bridges. Any project
or structure that leaves little room for error
requires the application of rigorous best practice
standards, particularly when it comes to data-
dependent, information-driven research, and analysis-
enabled projects with human lives at stake. These

practices ensure that the highest standards are upheld, minimizing risks and maximizing success in complex endeavors.

Credible and reputable standards are developed through a collaborative process that involves investigating, defining, integrating, and enhancing a specific collection of everyday work experiences. These experiences are then transformed into widely recognized frameworks and bodies of knowledge. These frameworks and bodies of knowledge are approved by a dedicated group of professionals who are committed to maintaining high standards. These standards are designed to address common challenges, utilize shared approaches, and employ effective methods and resources.

At the heart of successful information technology projects and processes are standards and practices defined by organizations such as the International Institute of Business Analysis® (IIBA), the Project Management Institute® (PMI), PeopleCert's Information Technology Infrastructure Library® (ITIL), Information Systems Audit and Control Association® (ISACA), and The Open Group Architecture Framework® (TOGAF).

In the construction industry, carpenters, electricians, plumbers, and machine operators play crucial roles. Likewise, certified automotive engineers and mechanics are essential for professional motor sports. Similarly, in Information Management, project management, business analysis, enterprise architecture, and IT service management are critical for success. The organization can achieve competitive success only when these crafts are consistently performed with a high level of excellence.

Embrace Emotional Intelligence. Emotional
intelligence (EI) describes the ability to recognize,
understand, and manage one's own emotions, as well as
influence the emotions of others. It involves using
emotions effectively to guide thoughts and actions
and build positive relationships.[4] The concept of
emotional intelligence was first introduced by
psychologists Peter Salovey and John Mayer in 1990
and popularized by journalist Daniel Goleman in his
1995 book *Emotional Intelligence: Why It Can Matter
More Than IQ*.

Imagine the expertise required to build the world's
tallest buildings, longest suspension bridges,
largest ships, safest automobiles, and fastest
trains. Consider the construction workmanship
demonstrated in ancient megaliths such as the
Egyptian pyramids, Mayan temples, and the Great Wall
of China. Think about the information that might have
been researched, captured, validated, communicated,
and used to accomplish these amazing feats. I can
easily imagine the improvement in management styles,
techniques, and approaches from the brutal and
tyrannical to some of the empathetic, insightful, and
sublime methods employed today.

At the heart of all companies are human beings, and
human beings are motivated by emotions. Are workers
motivated to perform their best through fear and
intimidation or from mutual respect, understanding,
trust, empowerment, and accountability? Do managers
demonstrate excellence through ridicule, public
shaming, or through positive reinforcement and the
use of discretion? Studies have shown that using

---

[4] Salovey, P., and Mayer, J. D. (1990). Emotional intelligence. Imagination,
cognition and personality, 9(3), 185-211. doi: 10.2190/DUGG-P24E-
52WK-6cdg

negative management techniques can lead to decreased motivation, lower job satisfaction, and increased employee stress levels, among other adverse outcomes. Positive reinforcement, such as recognition and rewards for good performance, is more effective in promoting excellence and improving employee engagement and productivity.[5]

The business imperative of emotional intelligence is to identify, influence, incentivize and promote those thoughts, actions, and behaviors that tend towards customer-perceived benefits and avoid (or at least minimize) behaviors that detract from the investor-realized value or threaten employee satisfaction. Therefore, the emotions and motivations that give rise to these behaviors must be observed, encouraged, and managed.

Furthermore, understanding the influence of internal and external emotional motivations in everything we do, experience, and see is crucial to understanding the Business Ultimatum. Emotions are the spark that sets the flame for our actions and behaviors, and emotional intelligence is an interpersonal asset beneficial to information managers.

Emotional intelligence has four main components: self-awareness, self-management, social awareness, and relationship management.[6] These components are essential for building professionally healthy relationships.

Using discretion, or making decisions based on individual circumstances, can be a valuable tool for

[5] Eisenberger, R., Stinglhamber, F., Vandenberghe, C., Sucharski, I. L., and Rhoades, L. (2002). Perceived supervisor support: Contributions to perceived organizational support and employee retention. Journal of applied psychology, 87(3), 565.

[6] Bradberry, T., and Greaves, J. (2009). Emotional intelligence 2.0. TalentSmart.

managers in promoting excellence and addressing individual employee needs. Effective management techniques should be based on a combination of personal and organizational factors and focus on building a positive and supportive work environment that encourages excellence and productivity.

Similarly, an emotionally intelligent team is particularly observant of specific signals conveyed by their choice of words, tone, attitude, facial expression, gestures, and those reflected by others. Therefore, information technology managers should strive to hire, train, and retain individuals with the primary interest, aptitude, and attitude to be a part of a self-aware, high-performance work team focused on delivering value to primary stakeholders. These team attributes can help to increase bonds of professional respect, effectiveness, and efficiency.

Filling the core trade professions with emotionally intelligent, interpersonally skilled craftspersons can help build an organization's resiliency, flexibility, and longevity. Employees and managers who are empowered to collaborate effectively across different teams, departments, and functions are better equipped to meet the inevitable problems, opportunities, and decisions required by the Business Ultimatum.

To Summarize, the Business Ultimatum encompasses various challenges that impact stakeholders' emotional, physical, and financial fulfillment. These challenges include emotional hurdles, economic obstacles, legal and regulatory requirements, competitive pressures, internal barriers, and financial obstacles. The Business Ultimatum forms the very foundation of survival for commercial organizations. To navigate this ultimatum successfully, knowledge workers, managers, owners, entrepreneurs, and investors must possess the necessary capabilities to rise to the occasion. The application of management science, the value derived from certified-professional trade practices, and advancements in emotional intelligence research and application are all crucial components that enable organizations to effectively address the challenges posed by the Business Ultimatum.

Galvanize the Data Quality Culture

Company culture refers to the collective attitudes, values, beliefs, language, and practices that define an institution or organization. It is similar to the cosmic microwave background radiation, a concept in astrophysics. CMB is a form of electromagnetic radiation uniformly present throughout the universe.[7] Similarly, culture binds societies, communities, and institutions together through shared beliefs, values, attitudes, language, habits, and practices. It creates a sense of unity and common identity within an organization or community.

In the corporate context, culture is the sum of common company beliefs, values, mission statements, and purpose manifested in organizational habits, team dynamics, managerial styles, projects, and business performance. Cultures reflect how employees interact, socialize within corporate communities, and develop strong professional working relationships between managers, co-workers, employees, vendors, and customers.

Each individual within an organization contributes to the overall company culture by bringing their own set of core beliefs, values, and attitudes shaped by their family, institutions, communities, and surroundings. These factors establish a foundation that influences how they respond and act in different work situations. Studies have demonstrated that when companies prioritize cultivating a positive work culture, they can boost employee morale, productivity, and retention rates. By fostering an

---

[7] National Science Foundation. (n.d.). Cosmic Microwave Background Radiation. Retrieved from https://www.nsf.gov/news/special_reports/cosmicmicrowave/

environment where employees feel valued and supported, organizations can create a more motivated and engaged workforce. This, in turn, leads to increased job satisfaction, higher productivity levels, and a greater likelihood of employees staying with the company for the long term.[8],[9],[10] For instance, Commonly accepted values and virtues for a great workplace include integrity, honesty, respect, fairness, trust, and collaboration. Companies that prioritize these values tend to have more engaged, committed employees who are more likely to remain loyal to the company. According to research, businesses can attract top talent and create a competitive advantage in the marketplace by fostering a positive work culture.[11],[12]

For businesses to create an excellent workplace environment for everyone, it's essential to focus on certain values and qualities. This involves evaluating, hiring, and retaining top-talent individuals who consistently exhibit the right characteristics and align with the positive dynamics of the organization's culture. Some of these values

---

[8] Harter, J. K., Schmidt, F. L., & Hayes, T. L. (2002). Business-unit-level relationship between employee satisfaction, employee engagement, and business outcomes: A meta-analysis. Journal of Applied Psychology, 87(2), 268-279.

[9] Saks, A. M. (2006). Antecedents and consequences of employee engagement. Journal of Managerial Psychology, 21(7), 600-619.

[10] O'Reilly, C. A., Chatman, J., & Caldwell, D. F. (1991). People and organizational culture: A profile comparison approach to assessing person-organization fit. Academy of Management Journal, 34(3), 487-516.

[11] Cameron, K. S., and Quinn, R. E. (2011). Diagnosing and changing organizational culture: Based on the competing values framework. John Wiley and Sons.

[12] Huang, L., and Hsu, C. W. (2016). The impact of organizational culture on the relationship between shared leadership and team creativity. International Journal of Human Resource Management, 27(8), 854-871.

include mutual respect and understanding, dependability, integrity, trustworthiness, teamwork, responsibility, self-motivation, perseverance, and emotional intelligence. By prioritizing these values, businesses can foster an atmosphere where employees feel respected, supported, and motivated to contribute their best efforts.

In any work environment, it's rare to find individuals who appreciate bosses who publicly yell at them, rely heavily on negative reinforcement, or lead through intimidation and fear. Similarly, most managers cannot tolerate disrespectful or dysfunctional employees within their teams, even if those employees deliver exceptional results. Effectively managing one's emotions is a crucial aspect of fostering a thriving business culture and promoting positive team dynamics. This highlights the importance of emotional intelligence in creating an environment that encourages growth and collaboration. By developing emotional intelligence, individuals can better navigate and regulate their emotions, leading to improved relationships, enhanced teamwork, and a more harmonious work culture.

An emotionally intelligent workforce is fertile ground to cultivate a practical, resilient company-wide data quality culture (DQC), measured by meaningful metrics that enable knowledge workers to support critical business functions and processes that build valuable products and services.

A healthy data quality culture promotes and incentivizes common standards of best practices and causal behaviors of data management to produce good outcomes and enables the highest, best use of information. It displays bulletins, posters, flyers, cup holders, Thermoses, and other swag promoting data quality around the office. It invests in core operational training and internal marketing campaigns that tie performance metrics to stakeholder fulfillment.

Effective data quality cultures conduct various activities to ensure their data is accurate, complete, and consistent. Some examples of these activities include:

1. Establishing data quality standards and guidelines to ensure that everyone understands what constitutes high-quality data.

2. Implementing data profiling and cleansing processes to identify and correct data errors, duplicates, and inconsistencies.

3. Conducting regular data audits to monitor data quality, identify issues, and take corrective action.

4. Providing data quality training to employees to help them understand the importance of data quality and how to maintain it.

5. Creating a data quality scorecard or dashboard to track data quality metrics and measure progress toward improvement goals.

6. Encouraging collaboration and communication among different departments and stakeholders to ensure everyone works towards the same data quality objectives.

7. Investing in data quality tools and technologies that can help automate data quality processes and provide real-time monitoring and alerts.

8. Assigning data quality responsibilities to
    specific individuals or teams in the
    organization to ensure that someone is
    accountable for maintaining data quality.

By conducting these and other similar activities,
organizations can establish a culture that values
data quality and takes the necessary steps to
maintain it.

Data Quality and Information Integrity have deep
roots in the Total Quality Management (TQM) movement,
stemming from the reconstruction of post-World War II
economies. TQM has a long history of success—
emanating from the early work of pioneering engineers
like Dr. William Edwards Deming and Walter Shewhart,
whose methods were used to help rebuild post-war
Japan. Their well-proven results led to the
development and application of the Plan-Do-Check-Act
model (PDCA) or "Shewhart Cycle" of Statistical
Process Control (Figure 1).[13]

Figure 1 - *PDCA Cycle*

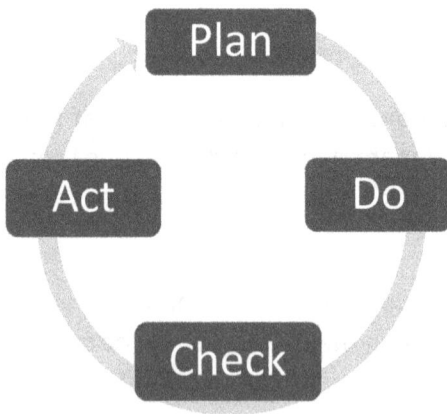

Recognizing that

---

[13] Walton, M. (1989). The Deming Management Method. New York, NY:
Perigee Books.

data is a product requiring quality controls and acting accordingly are essential to engineering a robust, resilient Information Management Engine (IME). IME strongly emphasizes process management as a sequence of interrelated activities that convert inputs (e.g., data and questions) into outputs (i.e., accurate decision and business intelligence). When poor-quality inputs are used, the resulting outcomes often lead to increased costs. This is because errors need to be identified and fixed to ensure accurate decision-making, problem-solving, and the ability to seize opportunities.

Subsequent advances in quality management took the form of modern frameworks and practices such as *ISO 9000*, an international quality management standard designed to help organizations build, maintain, and improve products and services; *Lean*, a systematic way to eliminate waste and enhance process flows; and *Six Sigma*, a set of tools and techniques designed to reduce the rates of defects produced by a process.

Just as TQM is essential to manufacturing, so is Total Data Quality Management to generating the information products of business processes. Information products—such as a customer master database, sales transaction history, and employee master data—have a distinct lifecycle the same as physical products, and they require careful controls to ensure the product is a complete, reliable, and trusted representation of objective facts.

Academic and professional organizations have published extensive research and literature on managing data and information quality. The MIT Sloan School of Management developed its Total Data Quality Management (TQDM) program in the early 1990s and evolved it into an information quality management

The Information Management Engine

program.[14] The Data Management Association's Body of Knowledge is another excellent resource for today's knowledge workers and data quality control personas to foster healthy, efficient data quality management cultures. [15]

My approach to managing data quality and information integrity is based on my 4 P's and T's Models (Figure 2). A data quality culture requires that **people**–knowledge workers, data engineers, data architects, and data quality analysts–receive practical **training** to build on their **talents** to fulfill the **purpose** of the data that is created and distributed into, within, and out of essential business **processes**. Process **performance** is a function of the organization's **technologies** and **techniques** and is consistently measured in meaningful, sustainable ways. All of these factors are surrounded and supported by **inspirational** leadership, **dedicated** professionalism, technology **innovation**, and **motivated** employees who see their success anchored in the health of the organization's data assets.

---

[14] Loshin, D. (2010). *Master Data Management*, p. 82. CITY: Elsevier Inc.
[15] Data Management Association. (2009). *Data Management Body of Knowledge* (2nd ed.). CITY: Technics Publications.

Figure 2- *The 4 P's and T's of Data Quality Culture*

Measuring data quality is vital to developing and growing a healthy data quality culture that strives to increase the value of data assets. The more a company needs accurate, complete, timely, reliable, and relevant data, the more valuable a data quality culture is for effective decision making, preventative problem solving, and enhanced opportunity realization.

Data Quality Management is an Ongoing Program

A robust data-quality management framework is an ongoing program anchored in

- accurate measurement systems,
- usage policies that guide decision-making and risk management,
- resilient workflow process performance, and

- information technologies and professional trade practices.

This framework is not limited to a particular project, work stream, or initiative. The program must persist across organizational changes, business disruptions, mergers, acquisitions, or divestitures.

Measuring Data Quality

Poor data quality can have negative business impacts, such as bad financial decisions due to inaccurate data entry, decreased customer satisfaction due to erroneous receipts, poor decision-making due to high levels of duplicate data, or decreased ability to prepare a product incomplete product. A robust measurement system of key performance indicators mitigates these issues.

Key performance indicators for data quality measure the *accuracy, consistency, completeness, uniqueness, conformity* to standards, *security* compliance, and *timeliness* of the data processing cycles through information technologies (Table 1).

Table 1 *Data Quality Dimensions*

Accuracy	Correctness of data and information compared to the source of record.
Completeness	Thoroughness of a given data set.
Uniqueness	Level of duplication in a given data set based on predefined data quality and business rules.
Consistency	Number of occurrences of accurate data entry and processing, which indicates the trustworthiness of a company's data.
Conformity	Degree to which data complies with predefined standards of format,

	type, length, and nullability.
Timeliness	Availability of the data when and where needed.
Security	Compliance with standards, policies, and regulations governing access.

Let's look at how these dimensions might play out in different scenarios.

Accuracy – Example: A customer places an order with a sales rep on January 22, 2024, and pays extra for rush delivery. The sales rep fails to include the request for rush delivery to the order entry clerk. The order is not accurate. Although this type of mistake seems minor, it can erode customer satisfaction and result in lost business if not corrected in time.

Completeness – Example: A database of driver's license holders must include each licensee's legal first and last name, current home address, proof of residency, and Social Security number. If the clerk forgets to enter the person's Social Security number, the database is incomplete. This can lead to major issues with validating the true identity, such as fraud prevention.

Uniqueness - Example: Data represents a distinctive object, fact, sign, or symbol. For instance, a Social Security number is unique to a given individual; a driver's license number uniquely represents a particular licensed driver. Duplicates in data can negatively affect the accuracy, usefulness, and reliability of decision-making, significantly impacting a company's reputation or business results.

Consistency – Example: A sales district manager wants to create an incentive program for the sales force. Consistently accurate data helps to ensure that compensation dollars are allocated based on actual performance. This gives business owners and managers confidence in the value of information.

Conformity – Example: Different business functions use the same data. Information about sales is used to fill orders (Sales), create invoices (Accounting), calculate profit and loss (Finance), determine who buys a product (Marketing) and whether new products are needed (Research). Conformity to a common format ensures the data maintains integrity across different information systems.

Timeliness – Example: In many businesses, data timeliness makes a tremendous difference to business results. For instance, Critical financial reporting and planning cycles (*usually at the beginning and end of the fiscal month, quarter, half, and year*) require timely and accurate data. For example, an exact accounting for a particular financial period means that all purchase orders must be entered into the computer system before the close of that period. Another example is the case of construction project managers' requirement for accurate architectural blueprints before completing a detailed project plan to coordinate the people and equipment needed to finish on schedule and budget. I am sure my readers can think of hundreds of additional examples where accurate data must be available within a critical time—especially in such industries as health care and defense, where lives are at stake.

Security – Example: How well a structured or unstructured dataset enables its intended purpose is a factor of its quality and security. This ensures data can be disseminated safely to those with a need-to-know, when and where they need to know it, without violating essential rules for code-of-conduct and usage.

Galvanize the Data Quality Culture

Setting Usage Policies

Data usage policies and standards help guide decisions, and owners and risk managers consistently ensure that information is used for its intended purposes in a manner consistent with regulatory obligations and standards of best business practice. Effective data policies are documented, communicated, shared, and enforced, enhancing an organization's chance of winning in the marketplace. These policies

- cover data movement practices and procedures from development to test to production in the system development lifecycle (SDLC)
- govern data privacy rights, and
- define the accurate labeling of official financial reports.

Organizations depend on data policies to minimize compliance risks and cost, reduce the cost of rework, enhance team collaboration, and improve productivity. For example, accounting organizations use Generally Accepted Accounting Principles (GAAP), a commonly accepted set of policies, concepts, and practices that facilitate transparency and consistency and minimize exposure to excessive legal fines or lost reputation.

Managing Data Quality Workflow

The data quality process encompasses the entire data supply chain, from creation to consumption and obsolescence. It includes the business rules governing data capture, update, usage, and deletion, as well as the data quality rules and edit checks that help enforce, monitor, and alert to violations of predefined thresholds. For example, data quality rules ensure that all sales orders contain total sales amounts (cannot be 0, null, or blank), sale date (mm/dd/yyyy format), unique customer identification (free of duplicates), and sales rep employee identification.

Data quality analysts and engineers program scripts that apply these rules to datasets, files, and databases. They ensure that data quality management processes and procedures are sufficiently documented, shared, audited, and maintained over time to keep up with internal and external changes. These document artifacts include Business Process Management Notation (BPMN) Diagrams, Responsible, Accountable, Support, Consulted, and Informed (RASCI) Diagrams, and others covering the Business Analysis Body of Knowledge© (BABOK).

The value of these artifacts is in not only the documentation of processes, but also the collaboration and synergy they facilitate between interdependent personas, teams, and organizations. Sales reps and marketing analysts depend on business intelligence analytics to help convert advertising campaigns into sales conversions; poor data-quality management processes significantly compromise this metric.

Like any critical business or technology process, data quality management must be sponsored from the top down and executed from the bottom up to ensure resilience and continuous improvement. The program must be shepherded through its maturity curve to advance the vital interest of the organization and increase and sustain the value of information assets. This is a critical responsibility of the chief information office and core to the Information Management Engine.

Establishing Information Technologies and Professional Trade-Practices

Galvanize the Data Quality Culture

Best-in-class data quality management is grounded in information technologies and professional trade-practices. This is particularly true for large- to-medium sized businesses. The sheer volume of data to be profiled for data quality, analyzed for the root cause of problems, remediated, and monitored often is too great for manual processing. With the advent of Big Data, unstructured objects from various data sources—including text, pictures, and video and audio—require robust application software platforms to measure and control data quality.

In addition, experienced trade professionals—such as data architects, IT developers, data analysts, and engineers—must acquire, build, or configure these software capabilities that deliver trustworthy data assets fit for the intended purpose. These trade professionals must be proficient at their craft to ensure the organizations' technology investments consistently deliver valuable investment capital returns, drive value creation, and deliver stakeholder expectations. We will spend more time exploring these personas in later chapters of this book.

Empower Keystone ITM Trade-Professions

Core information-management trade practices are vital to the success of data-driven organizations. Companies whose success depends heavily on data need high-performing trade practices in all their forms. Today's information technology management (ITM) professions include business analysis, project management, solution architecture, development and support, and, more recently, information governance and security. The keystone trade practices in ITM align with the six basic questions of what, why, who, when, how, and where (Table 2).

Table 2. Six Basic Questions in ITM

Profession	Six Basic Questions
Business Analysis	• What is to be delivered? • Why is this outcome important to stakeholders?
Project Management	• When will the expected value results materialize? • Who is required to deliver the change value?
Solution Architecture	• How will the solution be designed and architected?
Development and Support	• Where will the solution be delivered and serviced?

Business Analysis

The International Institute of Business Analysis®
(IIBA®) defines business analysis as "the practice of
enabling change in an enterprise by defining needs
and recommending solutions that deliver value to
stakeholders." [16] Change enablement can apply to any
business or information technology project, program,
portfolio, or process. The professional practice of
Business Analysis is documented very well in the
Business Analysis Body of Knowledge® (BABOK®),
published by IIBA. This globally recognized standard
and definitive guide informs the core tradecraft for
the Information Management Engine.

Business analysts—anyone responsible for the tasks
as defined by BABOK, regardless of their titles—work
in a wide variety of disciplines. Positions that
involve business analysis include systems analysts,
business process analysts, business architects,
product owners, business intelligence analysts, and
programmer analysts. Their tasks include

- understanding their organizations' goals,
  underlying problems, opportunities, and risks
- analyzing strengths, weaknesses, opportunities,
  and threats; then
- facilitating design solutions and strategies
  that address root causes, prevent problems,
  exploit opportunities, and mitigate risk.

The importance of business analysis can be traced
back to the early days of computer programming and
beyond. During the late 1980s and early 1990s,
programmer analysts recognized the need to better
understand the requirements of business computer
users and the programs they developed. It became

---

[16] International Institute of Business Analysis, *A Guide to the Business Analysis Body of Knowledge,* version 3, (Toronto: IIBA, 2015): 2

evident that the code created by programmers often did not address the end-users' needs, increase their productivity, or help streamline business processes to reduce costs and waste.

This realization led to the recognition of a gap between the needs of end-users and the solutions delivered by programmers. As a result, some programmer analysts started focusing on understanding, translating, verifying, and documenting the actual business needs of their customers. They became intermediaries between the information technology delivery teams and the business teams they supported. By bridging this gap and acting as liaisons, these analysts ensured that the technology solutions aligned with the true requirements of the business, resulting in more successful and valuable outcomes.

This evolution continues with today's business analysts, who facilitate stakeholder collaboration to fulfill the emotional motivations and needs of investors, business owners, customers, and employees. *It's important to always keep in mind the ever-changing needs and expectations of investors and customers, who are key stakeholders in any business.*

Primary Stakeholders are often driven by the need for specific emotional fulfillments, such as a feeling of accomplishment, a dedication to making a difference, a strong sense of ambition, the desire to change for the better, and many other emotions. These needs take different forms and layers:

- **Business requirements** encompass direct needs to deliver the Business Ultimatum, such as demonstrating return on investment, right-sizing product inventory levels, increasing sales volume, or decreasing product defect rate.

- **Emotional stakeholder requirements** are the motivations of customers and investors that lead them to choose an organization's products and services over competitors' offerings. These include the desire for premium product quality, the appeal of consistent rates of return, the expectation of preferential customer service or strong price sensitivities, and other driving emotions.

- **Functional requirements** describe the behaviors, features, and functions a solution must deliver to satisfy stakeholders' needs within a given context, interaction, or scenario. For example, "The system should allow the user to easily create and edit documents using a word processing software."

- **Nonfunctional requirements** comprise the quality, capacity, and performance expectations the solution must meet to deliver supportability, scalability, availability, and usefulness to stakeholders. For instance, "The system should have a response time of less than 2 seconds for any user interaction."

- **Supply-side requirements** entail the technologies, capacities, budget, human resource talent, and experience needed to deliver stakeholder perceived value and expected outcomes.

IIBA®-certified professional business analysts follow a framework outlined by six knowledge areas:
1. business analysis planning and monitoring,
2. elicitation and collaboration,
3. requirements lifecycle management,

4. strategy analysis,
5. requirements analysis and design definition, and
6. solution evaluation.

Each knowledge area breaks down specific tasks and activities necessary to achieve the expected outcomes. A professional business analyst knows to adapt this practice to the appropriate situation, project, or process. The knowledge areas are framework guidelines instead of strict rules to be followed under every condition.

These knowledge areas result from significant research, experimentation, and the collective experience of practitioners worldwide who strive to constantly improve and maintain the effectiveness of the business analysis practice. They accurately reflect collective insights into proven methods and means of delivering sustainable value for a change and serve as a guide to reassure those who depend on business analysts in various job titles to consistently demonstrate the capacity and ability to perform the critical tasks described in the BABOK.

I strongly encourage anyone inclined to practice business analysis to pursue the certification and drill into to the BABOK in detail for a thorough understanding of the practical value inherent in these practices.

Project Management

The art and science of getting essential things done are indispensable to the Information Management Engine; it's a critical cog in the machinery of value delivery. Practitioners have employed an evolving set of good practices, behaviors, and methods for the construction and development of monumental achievements over thousands of years. Consider the tradespersons involved in developing vaccines, chartering great universities, landing a man on the moon, or engineering works such as the Panama Canal or the great basilicas of Rome. Think about the transmutation of ideas to designs to completion and implementation. In every case, you'll find elements of structured, disciplined approaches and project management. Although many advantages were discovered by accident, most of those "accidents" happened within an initiative or project context.

According to the Project Management Institute (PMI), the globally recognized standard for the professional practice of project management, "a project is a temporary endeavor undertaken to create a unique product, service, or result." [17] In other words, project management is the art of getting things done within the constraints of sufficient access to time, money, technology, and talent. These constraints are essential to enabling the capacity and ability of project teams to plan accurate schedules, procure and develop technologies, and acquire skills and experience.

The Project Management Body of Knowledge® (PMBOK®), published by PMI, documents the continuous evolution of generally recognized standards of good practice to manage project processes that deliver value to stakeholders. It presents the essential practices and principles for project managers, from a system for value delivery to fundamental project management principles. These practices also are defined by the International Organization for Standardization (ISO 21500) and the American National Standards Institute (ANSI/PMI 99-001-202).

---

[17] Project Management Institute. (2017). *A Guide to the Project Management Body of Knowledge* (PMBOK Guide) (6th ed.). Project Management Institute.

The Information Management Engine

The ANSI/PMI standard's description of a value delivery system is particularly compelling for the Information Management Engine because the primary intent of IME is to deliver value realization to primary stakeholders. Customers, investors, business owners, managers, and employees depend highly on project managers to facilitate the transformation of investment capital for compelling project initiatives into the reality of expected outcomes and stakeholder perceived value.

The essential project management principles described in the second part of the standard are equally compelling in the effort to deliver stakeholder perceived value. Professional project managers must consistently demonstrate principle-centered behaviors that include:

- be a diligent, respectful, and caring steward

- create a collaborative project team environment

- effectively engage with stakeholders

- focus on value

- recognize, evaluate, and respond to system interactions

- build quality into processes and deliverables

- navigate complexity

- embrace adaptability and resiliency

- enable change to achieve their envisioned future state

The second part of the PMBOK is "A Guide to the Project Management Body of Knowledge," which documents performance standards for professional project managers. These include stakeholder performance, team performance, planning performance, project work performance, delivery performance, and measurement performance. Each of these domains is critical to the successful execution of a given initiative or change when tailored to meet the specific context and internal and external environment in which project management is practiced.

Like business analysis, project management employs several models, methods, artifacts, and techniques described in PMBOK 7th edition. Certified project management professionals bring these tools to bear in the execution of the Information Management Engine. Here are several standard project management methodologies and a brief description of each:

- **Waterfall**: A traditional, linear approach to project management that involves completing each project phase before moving on to the next.

- **Agile**: An iterative, flexible approach to project management that involves completing small increments of a project in short sprints, often with ongoing collaboration and stakeholder feedback.

- **Scrum**: An Agile methodology that emphasizes a collaborative, team-based approach to project management, with clearly defined roles and responsibilities, daily meetings, and ongoing reviews and retrospectives.

- **Kanban**: An Agile methodology that focuses on visualizing and optimizing the workflow through a project, often through a visual board that displays tasks and progress.

- **Lean**: A methodology that emphasizes minimizing waste and maximizing value through continuous improvement, often through visual management and Lean tools like value stream mapping.

- **Six Sigma**: A data-driven methodology that reduces defects and improves quality by identifying and eliminating process variations.

- **PRINCE2:** A methodology that provides a structured approach to project management, with clearly defined roles and responsibilities, detailed documentation, and a focus on continuous review and improvement.

Each methodology has its strengths and weaknesses, and the choice of methodology will depend on the specific needs and goals of the project and organization.

Professional project managers must demonstrate the appropriate subject matter acumen, leadership, and emotional intelligence required to facilitate expected outcomes. And they must have internal support from senior leadership, particularly the project management office, as well as external support from organizations like PMI® to enable their capability to perform.

I strongly encourage anyone inclined to practice project management, program or portfolio management to pursue the certification and drill into to the PMBOK in detail for a thorough understanding of the practical value inherent in these practices.

Solution Architecture

Solution architecture transforms ideas, dreams, aspirations, and hope into design options that solve root causes of core problems, enable accurate and timely decision-making, empower opportunity exploitation, and deliver the expected value to primary stakeholders. Again, consider the role of these practitioners in the design and development of impressive technologies such as the IBM Watson supercomputer, Amazon's Alexa Consumer Smart System, Facebook's Social Graph, Apple iPhone, and many, many others.

Solution architecture is separate from enterprise architecture, data, process or business architecture, though it relates to each of these. Its distinction is the function it plays in the project management processes. Solution architecture involves embedding problem or opportunity statements into projects in formal requirements; translating requirements into technical specifications; working with others to develop design options; selecting the preferred design; and working with the project team to develop, test, implement, and deploy the solution.

The Skills Framework for the Information Age (SFIA) defines solution architecture as the "design and communication of high-level structures to enable and guide the design and development of integrated solutions that meet current and future business needs. In addition to technology components, solution architecture encompasses changes to service, process, organization, and operating models." [18]

High-performance solution architecture teams mentor, develop and coach their top talent to achieve desired results within a project. This involves ensuring practitioners have access to training and certification towards globally accepted standards.

---

[18] Skills Framework for the Information Age, "Solution Architecture," SFIA-Online.org, accessed January 13th, 2023, from https://www.sfia-online.org/en/framework/sfia-7/skills/solution-architecture

One example is The Open Group Architecture Framework (TOGAF), a flexible and adaptable framework that can be customized to fit an organization's specific needs. It has become a widely adopted standard in the enterprise architecture community and is continually updated to reflect changes in technology and business practices.[19]

In my thirty-eight years of work experience on IT projects, solution architects have played a massive role in any project's prospects of being completed on time and within budget, headcount needs, and quality requirements. Large-scale digital transformations are a great example. A large manufacturing company embarked on a digital transformation to move from manual financial records into electronic data records with robotic process automation of specific clerical tasks. Our solution architects were pivotal to the success of this initiative. Our solution architects worked closely with business analysts to define and document requirements, with process engineers to capture critical workflow scenarios in business process diagrams, and with IT developers to build, automate and deploy the digitized financial records. This saved the company hundreds of thousands of dollars in overhead costs and positioned it to compete within its industry more efficiently.

Solution architects must be engaged in every stage of a solution's lifecycle. They help to assess the solution's health and improve its function from creation to maturity, maintenance, and decline to obsolescence. Empowering solution architects to

---

[19] TOGAF is maintained by The Open Group, a global consortium that develops standards and certifications for enterprise architecture, cloud computing, and other areas of IT. The framework is continually updated to reflect changes in technology and best practices. The Open Group's website URL is https://www.opengroup.org/.

perform at their best is vital to building a high-performing Information Management Engine.

Solution Development and IT Service Management

Core-critical to any information technology project is the role of development and support professionals. Since there are too many software and hardware technologies to mention, this section focuses on IT solution development and service management. As with the other professionals described above, those responsible for converting ideas, hopes, dreams, use cases, and requirements into real-world products and services are arguably most important to a high-performing Information Management Engine.

Whether configuring purchased software or building custom-coded solutions, developers convert ideas into digital or physical products and services to solve stakeholder problems, inform essential decisions, reduce uncertainty, and deliver primary stakeholder value. Depending on the technology, practitioners gain working knowledge through experience, training, and education; some pursue professional certification in software or hardware, including Microsoft, SAP, Salesforce, and Amazon Web Services (AWS). These certifications help business owners, investors, and organizations anchor their expectations of excellence on proven practice principles, methodologies, tools, and techniques from professionals and their sponsoring organizations. Project teams that accumulate and retain this top talent enable the performance of the rigorous processes and practices necessary to gain sustainable value through a common practice language and performance standards.

Organizations like AXELOS and PeopleCert provide proven certification frameworks designed to deliver stakeholder value—specifically the Information

Technology Infrastructure Library (ITIL), a globally accepted standard for information technology service management covering IT infrastructure components hardware, software, operating systems, networking, and communications. In addition, ITIL contributed to and aligned with the ISO standard for service management (ISO/IEC 20000) based on the British standard (BS15000).

ITIL originated from a library of more than 30 books developed during the 1980s by the Central Computer and Telecommunications Agency (CCTA) in Britain. It accumulated and codified best practices in information technology management, with input from the leading practitioners and organizations of the period.

In 2013, ITIL was acquired by AXELOS, a joint venture between the British government office and Capita, a UK outsourcing group. It sold ITIL to PeopleCert, a leader in the global assessment of information technology professional skills and development, in June of 2021. ITIL has been continually improved and streamlined, down to five books at the time of this writing in the form of version 4, which is focused on a set of seven guiding principles and four critical dimensions based on a holistic mindset anchored by an integrated view of the organization's value chain, called the service value system (SVS).[20]

ITIL 4 sets forth seven Guiding Principles:
1. **Start where you are**: Assess, understand, and appreciate the current state. Recognize the positives and build on existing strengths.

---

[20] ITIL 4 Foundation, Axelos, 2019, Chapter 2. The website for Axelos ITIL 4 is https://www.axelos.com/best-practice-solutions/itil.

2. **Progress iteratively with feedback**: Define the target state for the organization, then develop a transition plan and iterate through the critical path milestones, delivering incremental value toward the future state with stakeholder feedback from well-planned engagement.

3. **Focus on value**: Emphasize delivering returns on investment capital plus the cost of that capital, primary stakeholder perceived benefits, goodwill and reputation, regulatory compliance, and employee satisfaction.

4. **Collaborate and promote visibility**: Work with key stakeholders and IT trade professionals to demonstrate and advocate the benefits of applying the IT infrastructure Library of best practices.

5. **Keep it simple and practical**: Focus on the core practice and explain key details in simple, audience-appropriate language and terms. Stay focused on results and expected outcomes.

6. **Think and work holistically:** Understand the business environment and information ecosystem in the context of the overall organization. What critical business relationships and workflows are interdependent to the firm's success?

7. **Optimize and automate**: Apply lean principles to eliminate waste, document and streamline workflow processes and procedures; then and only then, automate where practical.

The ITIL 4 framework also includes the **four**

dimensions of service management, which help
organizations to take a holistic view of IT service
management, considering all aspects of the service
lifecycle:[21]

1. **Organizations and people**: An organization's
   roles, responsibilities, and culture that can
   impact service management. It includes
   leadership, governance, and employee skills and
   training.
2. **Information and technology**: The technology and
   information used to support service management.
   It includes designing, developing, and managing
   IT systems and applications.
3. **Partners and suppliers**: The relationships and
   collaborations with external partners and
   suppliers that can impact service management.
   It includes service level agreements, supplier
   management, and outsourcing considerations.
4. **Value streams and processes**: The end-to-end
   processes and workflows used to deliver
   services. It includes considerations such as
   service design, transition, and operation.

ITIL certification levels establish a benchmark for
performance, using accessible language, practical
methods, clear responsibilities, and specialized
skills for IT developers, engineers, analysts, and
scientists. This framework instills confidence in
business owners, consumers, investors, and
institutions, as they can rely on the expertise and
reliability of certified professionals. High-
performance information technology service management
acts as a force multiplier, enabling skilled
developers and helpdesk analysts to efficiently
deploy and maintain technology solutions. They can

---

[21] ITIL 4 Foundation, Axelos, 2019, Chapter 3.

address critical queries, convert opportunities into tangible value, mitigate risks, reduce uncertainty, and empower core IT professionals to excel in their roles.

Special Attention: Human Resource Management

Every employee, contractor, contingent laborer, or worker requires administrative support, training, direction, emotional encouragement, and advocacy to thrive and maximize their innate talents. This is especially true for those in pivotal roles in the organization, such as business analysts, process engineers, business intelligence specialists, project and program managers, solutions architects, data scientists, application developers, and support engineers. They are crucial to an organization's capability to deliver value to primary stakeholders. Therefore, those entrusted to manage, coach, develop and support information management practices have specific accountability to ensure these pivotal personnel have the capacity, ability, and desire to perform to best-practice standards. Direct-line managers, supervisors, directors, and senior-executives across all functions of an organization constitute the fulcrum upon which essential personnel and their capabilities to perform are balanced supply-to-demand.

Although Human Resources is responsible for employee support and administrative processes, their relationship with people managers can make or break an organization's ability to build and maintain an effective, efficient Information Management Engine equal to the challenge of their Business Ultimatum. For example, HR reps help people managers and supervisors to define job titles, roles and responsibilities, advancement levels, and career hierarchies, as well as collaborate with training departments to ensure key personnel have the proper education, training, and working-experiences necessary to deliver primary stakeholder value. They must ensure the organization has the right person and team in the right places at the right time to execute the right thoughts, behaviors, and activities necessary for a winning culture.

In my experience and research, Information management is a critical aspect of any modern business operation, enabling organizations to capture, process, store, and distribute information more effectively.[22] However, poor advocacy and support of information management personnel, processes and technologies can negatively impact business outcomes in some significant ways. For instance, if an organization fails to manage its data effectively, it may struggle to identify and respond to emerging trends, changes in the market, or customer needs. This can result in missed opportunities, and ultimately lead to a loss of competitive advantage.[23]

Another significant impact of poor information management is that it can result in operational inefficiencies. When an organization's data is not managed effectively, employees may spend significant time looking for the information they need to perform their jobs. This can lead to lost productivity, delays in completing tasks, frustrated employees, and ultimately, decreased overall business performance.[24]

Furthermore, poor information management can

---

[22] McLeod, R., and Schell, G. (2019). Management Information Systems (pp. 45-68). Pearson.

[23] Laudon, K. C., and Laudon, J. P. (2018). Management Information Systems: Managing the Digital Firm (pp. 91-112). Pearson.

[24] McLeod, R., and Schell, G. (2019), pp. 69-92.

negatively impact customer satisfaction. When customers cannot access the information, they need or experience delays in receiving services; they may become dissatisfied and less loyal to the organization. This can ultimately decrease revenue and negatively impact the organization's bottom line.[25]

There are several other examples of poor information management practices that can negatively impact business outcomes. One typical example is data silos, which occur when information is stored in different systems or departments, making it difficult to access or use. This can result in duplicate data, inconsistencies in information, and a lack of visibility into the organization's data.[26]

Another example of poor information management is the failure to secure sensitive information. The organization may face significant financial and reputational damage and legal liability in a data breach.[27]

Finally, ineffective information governance can also negatively impact business outcomes. Without clear policies, procedures, and standards in place, organizations may struggle to manage their data effectively, leading to inefficiencies and increased risk.[28]

Poor support, control, and oversight of information management processes, practices, and people can have a significant negative impact on business outcomes. Organizations that fail to manage these assets effectively may experience missed opportunities, operational inefficiencies, decreased customer

[25] Laudon, K. C., and Laudon, J. P. (2018), pp. 345-358.
[26] McLeod, R., and Schell, G. (2019), pp. 93-114.
[27] Laudon, K. C., and Laudon, J. P. (2018) pp. 610-625.
[28] McLeod, R., and Schell, G. (2019), pp. 115-132.

satisfaction, and other negative consequences. Organizations should prioritize information management, establish clear processes, policies, and procedures, and invest in the tools and human resources needed to manage their data assets effectively.

As a result, several organizations, like the **Society** for **Human Resource Management**® (SHRM®), highlight this crucial need to effectively manage the most critical resource asset in any organization, Human Resources. Certification organizations like SHRM provide a vital performance standard for these professionals to consistently demonstrate value to primary stakeholders and employees.

SHRM Certified Professionals establish a shared language, performance standards, and clear responsibilities when collaborating with personnel managers and supervisors. In certain situations, they may oversee or assist in implementing corrective actions that could result in terminations, demotions, or re-assignments of managers who fail to meet the essential needs of the business technology trade practitioners. Their aim is to empower these practitioners to effectively perform critical-path tasks, activities, and behaviors necessary for success.

Managing people is vital and should never be minimized, discounted, or underestimated! People come in a wide range of personalities, from those who are highly intricate and nuanced to those who prefer a more straightforward and uncomplicated approach. Additionally, individuals have their own unique mix of moods, styles, approaches, preferences, and cultural backgrounds. It's important to note that depending on the circumstances and the level of stress they encounter, anyone can exhibit a range of these complexities within a single day.

Skillful information technology managers know this and work hard with human resource personnel to balance the many challenges and rewards of helping others succeed within a given set of constraints. They are organized, dependable, creative, flexible, adaptable, and principle-centered in treating those they are entrusted to help grow, develop, and shine. Skillful IT people managers recognize the nature of business technology career choices and invite a variety of creative, disciplined, introverted and extroverted, sometimes stubborn, and inflexible personalities into the field.

People have distinguishing characteristics and personalities; therefore, the managerial challenge is leading them to successfully execute a set of proven practice standards, methods, and processes. Significant research, products, and services are available today to help maximize the value potential of core ITM Trade-Professionals.

For instance, Clifton Strengths-Finders was developed by Donald O. Clifton, a renowned American psychologist, businessman, and researcher, and published by Gallup Inc. Gallup, a research and analytics company focusing on employee engagement things. Gallup has developed a framework for employee engagement called the Q12 Survey, which consists of 12 questions that measure various aspects of employee engagement.

The Q12 Meta-Analysis Report summarizes the results of several studies that have used the Q12 Survey to measure employee engagement. According to the report, organizations that score in the top quartile on the Q12 Survey can see significant improvements compared to organizations in the bottom quartile. These improvements include a 7% - 23% increase in employee engagement, an 8% - 18% increase in productivity, a 22% - 48% increase in profitability, a 25% - 65% decrease in employee turnover, and a 37% - 59% decrease in absenteeism.[29]

These results suggest that deploying the Q12 Survey and using it to improve employee engagement can significantly impact organizational outcomes. With access to tools like these, Human Resource Professionals and ITM People Managers enable top talent within their teams to grow and develop into the skilled trade persons required for reliable Information Value Delivery.

Chapter Summary

Access to relevant, timely, reliable Information is an indispensable asset of any modern organization. Organizations must deploy high-performing teams of keystone ITM professional trades to ensure the organizations' Information Assets contribute to sustainable stakeholder value creation, complete employee satisfaction, continuous improvement, and competitive advantage. High-Performing ITM trade professionals are force multipliers critical to empowering modern organizations to maximize the value of their information assets. Specifically, Business Analysis, Project Management, Solution Architecture, Solution Development, and Support and Human Resource Management; developed, coached, and supported by highly effective People-Management.

These specific professions anchor critical process methodologies, standard operating procedures, policies, and practice principles of the Information

---

[29] Harter, J. K., Schmidt, F. L., and Hayes, T. L. (2002). Business-unit-level relationship between employee satisfaction, employee engagement, and business outcomes: A meta-analysis. Journal of Applied Psychology, 87(2), 268–279. doi: 10.1037//0021-9010.87.2.268

Management Engine necessary to exceed the Business Ultimatum. Business Technology Users depend on their working knowledge, skills, and experience to solve fundamental business problems, maximize decision accuracy, reduce uncertainty and risk, respond favorably to opportunities, and optimize strengths.

The keystone ITM trade practices are essential Value Drivers themselves, critical to increasing the Value of the Organization for Capital Investors, Stakeholders, and Owners in exchange for their Time-In-Effort, Rewards, Recognition, and Emotional Energy. Since Information Assets have both potential and actual value, they help convert potential information asset value into realized, real Value. Therefore, we'll cover Value Drivers and Stakeholder-Perceived Value Creation in the next Chapter.

Emphasize Value Delivery-Driven Data Management

Organizations need to align their core capabilities and resources related to Information Asset Management with Critical Success Factors, Key Performance Indicators, and Core Value Drivers. This is because primary stakeholders, including Customers, Inventors, Investors, and Business Owners, expect to receive value in return for what they consider valuable, such as their time, investment capital, working knowledge, and emotional energy. Defining, measuring, and creating meaningful cause-and-effect relationships that are perceived as valuable by these stakeholders is crucial. However, since the term "value" can have different interpretations, let's define it from two perspectives to provide clarity.

First, *"Value"* is the worth primary stakeholders place on their time, money, ideas, and emotional energy. They value things that are important to them, passionate about, and that are pivotal anchors and catalysts to their desired experiences, such as the Desire to send their children to College, the Aspiration to build a better World, the Dream to create World-Class Churches, Mosque or Synagogues, the Hope to travel the World, the Wish to cure Human Disease or the Dedication to build a World-Class Business.

Secondly, Value, from an economic perspective, is the financial worth of a good, product, or service in return for an equivalent item of value, merit, or substance. Such is the "Market Value" or "Valuation" of a Business or Asset if sold at Fair-Market Price. Specifically, the "Financial Valuation" process helps determine an organization's market value as measured by the performance of its Balance Sheet, Income Statement, Financial Ratios, and Future Discounted Cash Flows.

In the Value Based Management (VBM) framework, Value is created when the organization's Net-Return on Invested Capital incrementally exceeds the Cost of Capital invested. As Young and O'Bryne (2001, p. 5) stated, "Managing for Value involves managing the business with the objective of maximizing shareholder value. It means creating value for shareholders by earning more than the cost of capital. This requires a focus on value creation in everything the business does." [30]

In 1983, Stern Value Management, a New York-based Management Consulting Firm, developed the Economic Value Added (EVA) model for maximizing an organization's financial performance. Value is the Net Return on Invested Capital minus the Cost of Capital. According to Stern Value Management, the formula is

EVA = NOPAT − (Invested Capital * WACC) where

- **NOPAT** = Net Operating Profit After Taxes

- **Invested Capital** = Debt + Capital Leases + Shareholders' Equity

- **WACC** = Weighted Average Cost of Capital

EVA and Value-Based Management approaches are compelling in the hands of skilled professionals who understand when and where these applications are most appropriate and effective, especially when Certified Financial Planning and Analysis Professionals (FP&A)

---

[30] Young, S. D., and O'Byrne, S. F. (2001). EVA and Value-Based Management: A Practical Guide to Implementation. McGraw-Hill Professional.

are working closely with experienced Business Analysts, Project Managers, Solution, and Process Architects with a deep understanding of their industry, market, customers, investors, employees, partners, competitors and the critical-success-factors or value-drivers that add economic value to the organization.

Business Analysts, FP&A, Solution and Process Architects, and other professionals apply fundamental management science techniques, methodologies, tools, and practices to enable value creation by aligning core-critical Information Management capabilities to Critical Success Factors (CSF) Key Value Drivers. These approaches help ITM trade professionals identify, define, measure, analyze, and apply critical success factors to crucial value drivers at every firm level.

Key Value Delivery Cycles

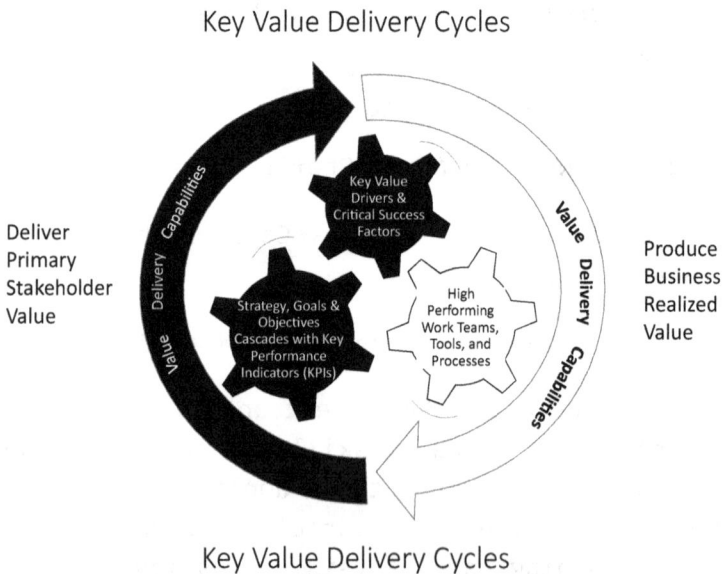

Key Value Delivery Cycles

Figure 3. *Key value delivery cycles of the Information Management Engine*

Emphasize Value-Delivery Driven Data Management

Critical Success Factors are all the Tasks, Behaviors, Resources, and Assets necessary to achieve Strategic Goals and Objectives. And *Key Value Drivers* are the most significant causal factors influencing the organization's capability to deliver Economic Value Add (EVA), Customer Perceived Value (CPV), and Return On Invested Capital (ROIC) and to achieve expected outcomes and objectives. A "Value Driver" is any variable that affects the valuation of the organization's total assets and financial statement, in addition, to delivering value to Customers, Investors, Owners, and Employees.

There must be a clear cause-and-effect relationship between the chosen measures and the statistical probability of value realization from the company's strategy. And a well-defined, high-performance standard for relevant trade practices, workflow processes, policies, and procedures and a value realization mindset in the organization's culture from Top-Down and Bottom-Up.

Many successful organizations manage key value drivers in the manner most appropriate to the Management Level, Business Unit, or Operation the value driver best fits. This ensures that all areas of the organization are aligned and focused on the value drivers that matter most to the business's success and that the value drivers are managed in a way that makes sense for each area.[31]

For example, Senior Executives focus on metrics like Company Growth, Profit- Margins, EVA, and other Financials metrics. At the same time, a Product Manufacturing Manager might focus on Defect Rates, Unit-Cost, and Cycle-Time. Or an Information

---

[31] Stewart, B. (1991). Economic Value Added (EVA) - The Real Key to Creating Wealth. New York: Simon and Schuster, p. 173.

Technology Manager might focus on High-Availability Computer Systems, Turn-around-Time for Support Tickets, Data Quality Defects, or Cybersecurity Risk Reduction.

In either case, the imperative is to validate which critical success factors are most determinate in accomplishing the organization's strategic goal cascades and objectives at every level. One of the techniques Business Analysts, Solution, and Process Architects use is Value Driver Tree Analysis alignment to essential Data Management Capabilities to ensure that Decision-Support and Data Science Models are focused on Value Creation.

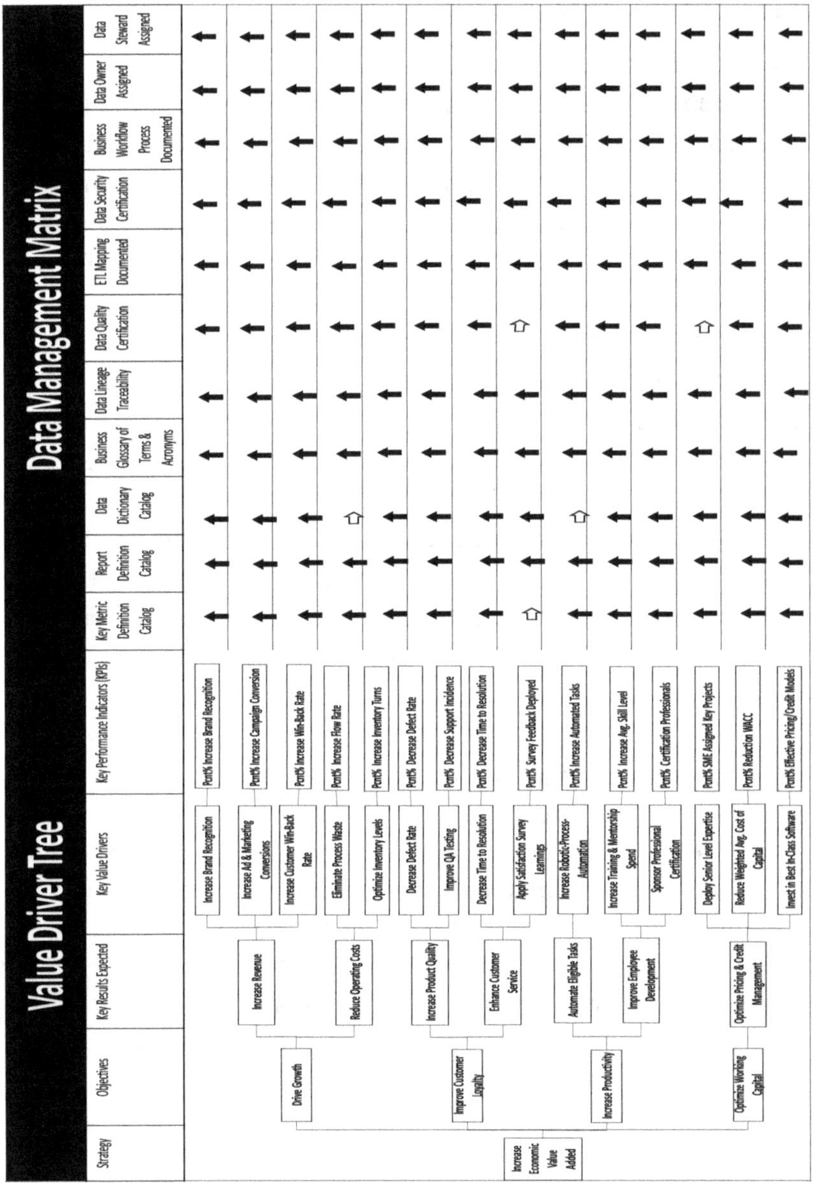

Figure 4 - Value driver alignment to data management

The Information Management Engine

Value Driver Tree Analysis

A value driver tree analysis is a visual diagramming exercise designed to elaborate value creation into cascading levels of causation, flowing from the strategic alignment of an organization's primary assets, technologies, and resources to key performance objectives and expected outcomes. Then, identify and validate the most robust cause-and-effect relationships between key value drivers to those objectives and expected results, enabled by a statistically valid set of critical success factors measured by a predefined set of key performance indicators (KPI).

These key performance indicators must be further broken down into the most critical data elements (CDE) requiring immediate attention from information technology-information management (ITM) professionals such as

- Data quality engineers, who ensure the KPIs are based on timely, relevant, complete, and accurate data free from duplication.
- Data security analysts, who confirm that sensitive data complies with all legal and regulatory obligations for cybersecurity.
- Business intelligence analysts, who ensure that KPI definition calculations are consistent and accurately measure the intended outcome.
- Senior data analysts, who ensure the data dictionary catalog, report catalog, key metric catalog, source-to-target mappings, and data lineage are documented, maintained, and accessible to the appropriate business units, lines-of-business, process owners, and data stewards who need them when they need them.

Emphasize Value-Delivery Driven Data Management

Align Data Management to Value-Delivery Controls

Targeted information management practitioners must align their core competency, time, and attention to the primary business objectives, key value drivers, and metrics the owners, managers, and leaders have defined to support actual, measurable information value realization. **Figure 4** describes such alignment between the value driver tree analysis and critical information management capabilities. Once the value driver analysis has been sufficiently completed and confirmed by statistically valid methods, such as correlation analysis using tools like scatter plots diagrams, information management practitioners align these critical capabilities to the Information Requirements of these value drivers. These capabilities must include the following:

- **Business Analysis Performance Management.** Excellence in business analysis performance yields a shared understanding between primary stakeholders, such as internal customers of Solution applications, and their crucial technology providers of the proper business needs, actual root causes of problems, or actual opportunities and threats identified and confirmed.

- **Project and Process Performance Management.** Excellence in project and process management performance delivers the required amount of organization, controls, coordination, and communication between project sponsors, teams, and technology providers necessary to achieve the business case and purpose of a given project's charter.

- **Key Metric Definition Catalog.** This catalog ensures a common understanding of the measures that drive actual value realization are documented, disseminated, and adopted throughout the organization. These detailed calculations and functions, embedded throughout the organization's code base, are often fragmented, uncalibrated, and unknown across different technology and analytics teams in medium to large organizations.

- **Top Report Definition Catalog.** This catalog documents critical reports and dashboards supporting the organization's most essential operations and functions. Organizations must be vigilant regarding change impacts on these reports; unintended consequences can lead to inaccurate, unavailable, and unreliable decision support. For instance, an operating system upgrade should lead to regression testing of all critical reports dependent on that operating system.

- **Data Dictionary Catalog.** This catalog anchors a shared understanding between technology providers regarding essential information about the data key performance metrics depend on, such as technical data definition, format, type, length, and sample values. These are particularly important for data integration and migration projects to ensure the mapping is consistent and conforms to data policies and Standards.

- **Data Quality and Business Rules Catalog.** The most critical data in the organization must comply with a standard set of data quality and business rules to achieve the highest and best use of the purpose of that data. These data quality rules will cover such critical dimensions as accuracy, uniqueness, conformity to format standards, consistency, accuracy, and timeliness.

- **Business Glossary of Terms.** In large- to medium-size organizations, it helps to ensure a common understanding between functional teams, processes, and projects. These include the definition of commonly used acronyms, business process notation, and industry-specific, widely used words. As a result, the business glossary of terms should be made easily accessible to all practitioners required to have a common understanding and share a common business language, such as those in the healthcare industry, auto manufacturing, or the aerospace industry.

- **Value-Delivery Workflow Process Certification.** This certification is essential to ensure value-delivery work is well defined, organized, streamlined, and optimized to reduce waste and produce expected business outcomes. Business process management and data ownership practitioners are accountable for ensuring that high-quality, reliable data management practices support value-delivery workflow. Certifying and auditing these practices against rigorous standards is a critical success factor of the organization's ability to deliver essential value drivers.

- **Data Lineage-Traceability Mapping.** Data management teams must be able to plan change impacts effectively, reduce data discovery cycle time, increase the accuracy of robotic process automation, artificial intelligence, and machine learning algorithms. Mapping improves the success rate of digital transformation initiatives.

- **Data Architecture Certification.** Data should be designed and architected to fit the business purpose it is intended to deliver, its highest and best use. Practitioners who consistently apply rigorous standards of best practice help to assure their organizations that their Information Asset Management is built upon the most solid foundation possible to ensure value realization.

- **Data Quality and Security Certification.** Organizations must ensure that data quality rules and security policy enforcement, essential to reliable Information asset management, conform to rigorous standards. This certification practice helps ensure decision-making is based on objective facts, problem-solving is addressed at the source, and risk reduction activities are preventative.

- **Data Processing Alerts and Notification.** Data processing operations should conform to service-level agreements (SLA) between IT and business teams and operating-level agreements (OLA) between IT-to-IT teams. They are always on when and where needed to support value-delivery supply chains.

- **Data Stewardship Center of Excellence.** Data stewards provide accountability for the overall health, usage, and value of critical data assets in the hands of essential subject matter experts. Data stewards can be either IT or process personnel with particular or general responsibilities for data-dependent activities in the organization. Many leading organizations, such as business data analysts and data science engineers, build and analyze specific core competencies to perform these functions. The COE may comprise a combination of roles or personas across a community of practice focused on ensuring that vital information assets are fit-for-purpose and put to their highest and best use.

Chapter Summary

Value delivery is the capability to galvanize, enable and align the essential assets of an organization to produce the expected outcomes of primary stakeholders and supply-side enablers. Data and information are among the most critical of these assets. Information value realization is paramount to optimizing all business assets and depends on the performance of essential information technology and business process practitioners, methodologies, and best practice standards.

Organizations that consistently and effectively invest in the critical success factors of sustainable value creation have strong positions in their respective marketplaces and tend to adapt to change for long-term success. Organizations like Procter and Gamble, AT&T, Northrop Grumman, IBM, Hewlett-Packard, Archer Daniels Midland, and many others illustrate the capability to perform through effective use of business intelligence information and the critical data foundations underneath. Therefore, our focus

The Information Management Engine

shifted to a high-level review of particular data dimensions to achieve the highest and best use of the information asset.

Inspire the Highest and Best Use of Data Assets

All organizations rely on some form of data to drive their operations, functions, research and development, processes, and workflows. From the information age to digital transformation, data requirements often determine the success or failure of an organization's critical investments in technology or process projects, programs, and initiatives.

Data is invaluable to the success of digital transformation initiatives, such as robotic process automation (RPA), artificial intelligence (AI), the internet-of-things (IoT), and machine learning (ML). These innovations can lead to competitive market advantage, significant reductions in the cost of goods sold, an increase in the economic market value of an organization, and improved economic value added or consequential losses, waste, and rework if the critical data inputs are not managed with excellence.

Therefore, an organization's data must be put to its highest and best use possible under a given set of constraints. The highest and best-use concept was first introduced in the mid-1800s to early mid-1900s to appraise the actual property's market value. The Appraisal Institute defines highest-and-best use as the "reasonably probable and legal use of vacant land or an improved property that is physically possible, appropriately supported, financially feasible, and that results in the highest value." [32]

---

[32] Appraisal Institute. (2019). The Appraisal of Real Estate (15th ed.). Chicago, IL: Appraisal Institute. Retrieved from

The Information Management Engine

The concept of highest-and-best use from real estate can be applied to data asset management by considering the most effective and valuable use of data assets within an organization.

Just as vacant land or an improved property can have different potential uses that may result in different values, different data assets within an organization can have different possible uses that may result in additional value-creation opportunities.

For example, suppose an organization has collected a large amount of customer data through various sources, including online transactions, surveys, and social media platforms. The highest-and-best use of this data asset would be to identify patterns and insights that could be used to improve customer experiences, inform product development, and ultimately drive revenue growth.

However, if the organization is not using the data effectively or protecting it adequately, the data's value may be diminished. In this case, the highest-and-best use of the data would be to invest in better data management practices, such as data governance and data security, to ensure it is used appropriately and protected.

This concept should be applied to data valuation relative to an organization's mission, vision, strategy, and goals. To realize their most significant economic value, data assets must be fit for purposes that are technologically possible, reasonably probable to deliver expected benefits, reliably supported by IT operations, cost-effective, financially feasible, and result in the highest

---

https://www.appraisalinstitute.org/the-appraisal-of-real-estate-15th-edition/

economic return on investment in its creation, storage, retrieval, application, expiration, analysis, and usage.

This is the mindset that data management professionals must have to ensure measurable, meaningful value is delivered to the organization's primary stakeholders and empowers the organization's critical value enablers, change agents, high performers, and producers. Data management practitioners, in particular, must be proficient in the efficient use of data categories and classifications according to their potential contribution to value creation. Categories (Table 3) are defined by the purpose of the data; classification (Table 4) is based on who should be able to access it. Information management practitioners, data stewards, and owners must pay particular attention to the management, quality controls, monitoring alerts, and notifications needed to ensure maximum benefit from these essential data assets.

Table 3. Data Categorization

Category	Description	Examples	Type of data
Master Data	Essential-core data requires a commonly shared usage definition across the organization—specifically, unique identifiers, taxonomies, and hierarchies, along with their qualifying attributes. Master data typically includes unique customer IDs, product IDs, geo location IDs, employee identifiers, and a few	Customers, products, geographic locations, calendar/time, services	Structured Data
Reference Data	Essential-core data requiring a commonly shared usage definition across the organization; typically, slow to change over time. These are generally data elements whose names contain the keywords *code*, *list*, *type*, or *category* – in other words, things that would go in a dropdown list on a computer screen and require unique descriptions.	Product type, account type, order type, delinquency code, iso country codes, sales account hierarchy, chart of accounts, reason codes, job codes, cost center codes, profit center code	Structured

Category	Description	Examples	Type of data
Transaction al Data	Core-critical, event-driven data, typically resulting from business interactions involving an element of date/time, numerical value, and an object of value to one or more people. It demands a high degree of data quality, governance, and security to achieve the highest and best use for the	Point-of-sales, invoices, purchase orders, sales orders, returns, receipts, payments, shipments	Structured
Operational Data	Data is produced by an organization's day-to-day operations, equipment, and processes. Such as the number of units produced, the number of boxes shipped, labor hours worked, product defects returned, the number of loans approved, the	Sensor data, inventory data, shipping data, receiving data, factory floor data, admissions data, satellite data	Structured or Unstructured

The Information Management Engine

Category	Description	Examples	Type of data
Financial Data	Core-critical finance and accounting data records contained in ledgers, journals, statements, and file folders are organized, managed, tracked, and audited following legal regulations and standards of business conduct.	General ledger, income statement, cash flow statement, accounting journals, accounts payables, accounts receivables, payrolls, budgets	Structured
Analytica l Data	Transformations of raw data into information, understanding, insight, or intelligence concerning a particular object, question, problem, or opportunity. It is used to make decisions, solve problems, or answer critical questions regarding a given set of scenarios, conditions, or constraints.	Market analysis, benchmarks, data science models, diagrams, charts, surveys, laboratory research, sentiment analysis, swot analysis, root-cause analysis, pareto analysis, RASCI	Structured or Unstructured

Category	Description	Examples	Type of data
Organizational Data	Essential data that describes the structure and elements of an organization, its critical operating policies, procedures, and documents. It is typically associated with human resources, organizational change management or training	Policies, procedures, contracts, statements-of-work, legal documents, org charts, job level hierarchies, job titles and descriptions, training courses and curriculum and	Structured or Unstructured
Metadata	Data about other data, e.g., data documentation, to document a shared definition and understanding of a particular object, process, condition, or element of objective fact. Metadata can take	Data catalog, data dictionary, data flow diagrams, data models, data mapping documents, data lineage, architecture diagrams, metric definition catalog,	Structured or Unstructured

Table 4. Data Classification

Classification	Description	Examples	Type
Public	Data readily available for general-purpose use.	Court records, news feeds, press releases, public university courses	Structured or Unstructured
Private	Data that can be used, either solely or in combination to identify a person, family, or household uniquely; requires strict controls and governance at the risk of significant potential fines, loss of	Social Security number, taxpayer ID, medical record identifiers, computer network IP address, home phone number, bank account number, credit card number, phone records, or tax records	Structured or Unstructured

Classification	Description	Examples	Type
Confidential	Information requires discretion within an organization, team, or individuals. This data can also be shared between organizations in a business arrangement, typically requiring a legally binding nondisclosure agreement. Unauthorized disclosures can damage an organization's	Individual salary amounts, certain organization decisions, price lists, product research, sales strategy documents, nonpublic financial statements, and personnel records	Structured or Unstructured
Restricted	Data characterized by a need-to-know basis only; tends to provide market advantage, unique value proposition, or competitive edge, requiring the strictest of controls at the risk of significant legal penalty, fines, employment termination, or arrest.	Specific formulas or recipes, military or government secrets, insider trading information and particular intellectual capital, and attorney-client privilege.	Structured or Unstructured

The Information Management Engine

Control Master and Reference Data Identifiers

Master data management (MDM) is the set of processes that control the management of master data values to enable consistent, shared, contextual use across systems of the most accurate, timely, and relevant version of the truth about essential business entities.[33] MDM involves implementing necessary controls over the critical content values and identifiers that enable consistent use, shared understanding, and the most accurate representation of the essential business entities within a given context. For example, conflicting versions of a customer's preferences, purchases, returns, or satisfaction scores can erode the organization's customer base; inaccurate roll-ups and summaries of the organization's financial data if customer information is ambiguous or duplicated.

Similarly, *reference data* is any data used to organize or categorize other data or for relating data to information within and beyond the boundaries of the enterprise.[34] (DMBOK, 2017, p. 354). Reference data usually consist of codes, descriptions, or definitions and contain keywords like "List," "Type," or "Code" in the name of the data element. *Reference data management* (RDM) is the process that controls standard lists of values and content needed to ensure consistent usage, accuracy, and conformity of metadata data across the organization's operations, functions, and business units.

Data analysts, business analysts, data stewards, and custodians are essential in maintaining reference data's integrity and relevance to enforce its fit-

---

[33] Data Management Association International. (2017). Data Management Body of Knowledge, 2nd ed. (Tampa, FL: Technics Publication), 354.
[34] Ibid.

for-purpose standard. Reference data often drives the workflow process logic in organizations, depending on a given set of assumptions, scenarios, or conditions. These include a list that must be actively maintained, like job title codes, cost center codes, profit center codes, ISO country codes, ISO state codes, product type codes, geography codes, reason codes, sales area codes, ZIP codes, telephone area codes, etc.

Imagine how difficult it would be to optimize an organization's resources and processes without sufficient maintenance reference data. Unfortunately, many organizations don't have to imagine it; instead, they live it every day — the pain points and the frustrations! Information management professionals must remedy and prevent these pain points from occurring.

Validate Transactional, Operational, and Analytical Data

Business transactions and the operations that drive them generate the most important data for any commercial organization. This data is crucial for meeting the Business Ultimatum and fulfilling the emotional needs of the organization's primary stakeholders: investors, employees, and customers. Transactional and operational data serve as vital inputs for advanced analytics, data science, and business intelligence. They form the foundational elements of the data supply chain, fueling the organization's value-delivery engine and enabling continuous improvement feedback loops. Consequently, it is essential for the organization to empower information management professionals to ensure that critical business data transactions, inputs, and outputs are accurately captured, stored, transmitted, transformed, aggregated, validated, supported, and maintained.

The consequences of not performing these activities with excellence are insidious. They can lead to dramatic dysfunction, disharmony, and negative disruption between business units, project teams, and individuals in the form of internal strife, political mistrust, and blame, not to speak of inaccurate financial statements, poor decisions making, and ineffective problem-solving. The roots of such problems can grow long and deep in an organization and typically requires significant investment to rectify after the fact.

Prioritize Metadata Management

Much like document management, metadata management must be more understood and managed. its importance seldom rises to the awareness of senior executives, project and program managers, IT developers, and architects. It is often viewed as low-priority overhead work that contributes little value to the data supply chain.

In reality, nothing can be further from the truth. An objective assessment reveals the criticality of metadata and document management in reducing an organization's legal and financial risk; increasing the success rate of digital transformation initiatives; reducing project cycle time and, therefore, the cost of data discovery; increasing knowledge sharing between IT developers and architects; improves shared understanding between business end-users and IT developers; flowing traceability for critical data assets to business value drivers, key performance indicators, and critical success factors — all of these benefits of metadata help to facilitate the attainment of key objectives and goals.

Metadata includes information about technical and business processes, data quality rules, business rules, business workflow process diagrams, critical data pipelines and governance of the data diagrams, architecture infrastructure models, and diagrams. According to DAMA DMBOK[2], "Metadata helps an organization understand its data, systems, and workflows. It enables data quality assessment and is integral to managing databases and other applications. It contributes to the ability to process, maintain, integrate, secure, audit, and govern other data."

A helpful analogy of the general attitude toward metadata and document management is walking into a dark room and flipping the light switch. If the lights come on, you don't give it a second thought; the minute the light does not turn on, you notice immediately. Similarly, organizations generally value metadata and document management only after a crisis, such as a failed legal audit.

Organizations depend on information management practitioners that grasp the importance of managing metadata and critical documentation, despite these common misperceptions or significance or lack of senior leadership prioritization and support.

Chapter Summary

All business organizations heavily depend on data asset management. Data assets come in a variety of categories and classifications. Information management practitioners must be faithful stewards of the organization's trust in their capabilities to perform all the necessary functions and tasks to maximize the highest and best use of the organization's data.

The Information Management Engine

High-performance data asset management is an
essential element of the Information Management
Engine's ability to meet the Business Ultimatum and
successfully fulfill the emotional and financial
needs of primary stakeholders, customers, and
investors.

Prioritize IT Investment Economic Value Added

Investing in information technology infrastructure can be a substantial expense for an organization, especially when it includes ongoing software licenses and the need for temporary or permanent technical support and development personnel. Therefore, it is crucial to align these expenditures with the goal of delivering value to investors and equipping internal knowledge workers with the necessary tools to provide value to end customers. Managers responsible for maximizing the return on invested capital for data assets play a vital role in enabling and sustaining these capabilities.

Information Technology Infrastructure ROIC

Information technology infrastructure is a core-critical imperative of all the value-delivery capabilities described above. It is essential to enable organizations to make the most of the intellectual-electricity capacitors available. Information technology, in all its forms, is the competitive imperative for today's Business Ultimatum.

Organizations with the most resilient, adaptable, scalable information technology investments more quickly and efficiently respond to changes in business priorities. Factors driving the need for rapid change include shifting economic conditions, emerging competitive pressures, and many other disruptive events, threats or weaknesses.

Furthermore, organizations with high levels of data

quality controls, value-centric data governance, and efficient master and reference data management processes more easily leverage artificial intelligence, machine learning, natural language processing, and robotic process automation innovations. This is especially true of those firms employing the professional proficiencies required to ensure these investments' return on capital exceeds the cost of that capital.

To maximize this potential, information technology professionals must continually improve their proficiency at translating technology investments into returns on invested capital exceeding the cost of that capital for sales, marketing, product development, or any of the primary products and services that a given business offers.

Imagine your direct-line manager asking you to lift 1,000 pounds over your head. You would almost certainly reply that you do not have that capability. If that same manager asked if you could lift 1,000 pounds over your head using a forklift and proper training, your response would be quite different.

Information technology infrastructure investments must be viewed as a similar enabler, especially given the rapid advancement in microprocessor capacity; business workflow innovations, like Lean IT, Six Sigma, and Agile Project Management; and cloud-based computing, such as Platform-As-A-Service (PaaS), Infrastructure-As-A-Service (IaaS) or Software-As-A-Service—all of which offers capabilities on demand.

IT trade-practice professionals, in partnership with financial planning and analysis professionals, are critical links in the value delivery train of analyzing investment options, providing recommendations, and delivering decision support to IT Infrastructure choices. The business case to proceed with an investment or not must yield the organization the right technologies, processes, and policies needed in the moments that matter most to their primary stakeholders when required.

Whether it be a capital expenditure like purchasing new hardware servers or an operating expenditure like paying an annual cloud-software usage license, the business case must demonstrate a return on invested capital (ROIC) for a particular infrastructure project and show a direct link to the organization's critical success factors, key value-drivers, objectives, and key performance indicators. The Information Management Engine Value-Delivery Model supports, promotes, and advocates for core IT-trade practice professionals to build these skills over time and exercise the mental and emotional muscles necessary to demonstrate proficiency in IT infrastructure ROIC and EVA. This often leads to decisions regarding IT infrastructure buy-versus-build analysis.

The decision to buy versus build information technology is vital for organizations, which must be taken with due diligence and careful consideration. There are essential tradeoffs, pros, and cons to each approach.

By building information technology, the organization can deploy software engineers — working with business analysts, solution architects, and other IT professionals — to craft customized solutions designed to meet very particular needs for particular scenarios unique to a given set of business experiences. This helps to understand and document the need at the root-cause level in order to resolve fundamental problems and exploit business opportunities.

In contrast, purchasing information technology

takes advantage of a marketplace of tremendous innovations designed to deliver critical features and functions that meet the most important functional and process requirements in a given business. There is an impressive marketplace of cloud and on-premise solution offerings to support accounting, finance, manufacturing, sales, marketing, or any of the traditional functions within an organization. These configurable solutions are designed to address the most common problems, weaknesses, and threat scenarios typically encountered by traditional business units and functions.

In addition, more specialized technologies are available designed to deal with niche requirements such as data governance, data quality, metadata management, and nonfunctional requirements that a business analyst and solution architect typically leads an organization through. Nonfunctional requirements describe service-level needs for workflow process speed, CPU capacity forecast, and data security.

When weighing buy-versus-build, IT trade professionals often engage third-party consultants with particular expertise in this business case analysis. They employ analytical techniques like Decision-Tree Analysis, Value-Driver Analysis, Comparative-Analysis, and SWOT analysis to determine the relative strengths, weaknesses, opportunities, and threats that may determine the organization's readiness for one option or the other. This analysis will often lead to Requests-For-Proposals (RFP) or request for quotes from different vendors to compare their estimates to the cost and effort to custom-build a solution that meets the prevailing needs.

Figure 5 depicts a high-level comparison of different vendors' software. Each function or feature of the software is evaluated against a description of the organization's requirements for that function. The possible scores range from 1 to 5, with 1 being the Likelihood that the software *"Barely Meets"* the needs, 3 is *"Moderately Meets"* and 5 is *"Strongly Meets."* In this hypothetical example, Vendor #5 and Vendor #4 have the highest ratings, so they would be invited to submit a quote for their pricing and support packages to determine the final vendor selection.

Functionality Category	High Level Requirements	VENDOR #1	VENDOR #2	VENDOR #3	VENDOR #4
Data quality profiling	Ability to investigate the current state of data in a database or data set and determine the the business engagement approach to sanctioning and certification completeness, uniqueness, conformity, timeliness, accuracy, consistency, and referential integrity	3	2	4	4
Data transformation	Ability to transform common datatypes to meet established standards and policies (states, codes, numbers, names, etc..)	4	5		5
Data standardization	Ability for data stewards, data analysts, data architects, developers, and business analyst to create logical components from free-form fields, generally name and address	3	5	4	3
Data match and merge (exact and fuzzy)	Ability to identify and match duplicate records based on exact or fuzzy logic, with the ability to define gold standard record based on robust survivorship rules				5
Data validation	Ability to measure key data quality results as determined by key data quality dimensions: completeness, uniqueness, conformity, timeliness, accuracy, consistency, integrity			5	4
Data quality KPI scorecard & reporting	Ability to create, track and report the data quality health metrics/KPIs by essential dimensions of by essential dimensions			4	4
Data quality monitoring and email notification	Ability to trigger email notifications to data management personnel when established data quality thresholds are breached		3	5	3
Metadata catalog – data dictionary management	Ability to connect to a target data source, scanned the metadata schema and automatically create the data dictionary catalog	4	4	5	
Business data glossary management	Ability to create and maintain an ongoing list of standardized and commonly used business terms and definitions to enable business process standardization and common understanding	3	4	4	3
Business rules inventory management	Ability to inventory essential, standardized business rules for handling data that must be applied to business process activities that depend on the health of that data	3		4	
Data lineage source – two – consumption tracking	Ability to trace data journey from original source to the final destination including metric calculations ETL logic and any other data manipulations	2	4	3	
Mailing address validation	Ability to correct and validate any address to USPS standards	4			4
Email address validation	Ability to correct and validate email addresses to commonly accepted internet standards	4			5
Total Score		30	27	38	40

Figure 5 - *Data Governance and Quality Management Vendor Comparison*

Although Figure 5 is a hypothetical example, it highlights the need for IT trade professionals and their key business partners to invest due diligence in time, analysis, planning, and execution to enable the organization to ensure that information technology infrastructure investments deliver return on invested capital at a rate exceeding the cost of the invested capital.

Chapter Summary

Information technology investment can be a significant budget line item. CIOs and senior IT leaders must demonstrate quantitative and qualitative evidence of return on invested capital. This challenge is substantial and requires creativity, objectivity, diversity of thought and open-mindedness. Fortunately, advances in analytics, machine learning, and artificial intelligence can help. These innovations must be leveraged by IT for internal analysis of correlations and causation of information technology ROIC. Though we realize correlation does not necessarily imply causation, insightful IT leaders take on the challenge of searching for empirical evidence to demonstrate the financial and productivity benefits of IT investments.

PART II: Perform Information Value-Delivery

Information is the Primary-Need of all living Organisms and the Organizations they form. It enables the acquisition and fulfillment of all other basic survival and growth needs when acquired, perceived, processed, understood, and applied by the time and place of need.

As a result, the correct information at the right time, place, and amount provides enormous potential value to its owners and consumers. It can add a competitive edge to any Organization, School, or Business seeking advantage in their marketplaces of choice when acquired, processed, stored, and distributed more efficiently and effectively than others.

Therefore, the objective of Professional Information & Technology Management Trade-Practices, such as Project and Process Management, Business Analysis, Solution Architecture and Design, IT Development, and Human Resource Management, is to Transform Information Value-Potential into Realization of its Maximum-Value-Potential, Highest-and-Best-Use and measurable, Information Value-Delivery.

The primary purpose of *The Information Management Engine* is to describe a system of interconnected Trade-Practice Performance designed to provide the Information Value-Delivery required to meet the Business-Ultimatum defined in this work.

The Information Management Engine™

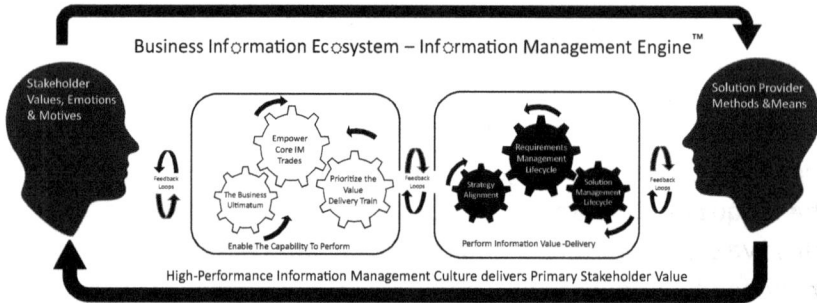

Figure 6 - *Information Management Engine Value-Delivery Model*

Overview

The Information Management Engine is a Value-Delivery Ecosystem of Continuous Improvement Feedback Loops, Professions, Processes, Tools, and Techniques of Applied Management Science, anchored in the creation and care for a Culture of Performance Excellence driven by pivotal Information & Technology Management Trade-Practices; whose core design-intent is to deliver primary-stakeholder perceived value in exchange for an equivalent or greater worth.

The Engine is powered by a strong set of Stakeholder Emotions and feedback loops that drive Strategy Alignment throughout the organization. These loops encompass the lifecycles of Requirements and Solution Management, which are essential for building and sustaining the delivery of valuable information. They enable the organization to fulfill its Strategic Goals, Objectives, Mission, and Vision, as these capabilities are necessary prerequisites for achieving them.

Once the organization's strategy is defined, senior leadership must buy or build the capability to achieve its strategic purpose. These core-critical capabilities are necessary for the value of an Information Asset to remain dream-deferred. Therefore, due diligence must be applied to aligning the organization's most critical capabilities to the Requirements and Solution Management Professions, Processes, Tools, and Techniques necessary to fulfill their primary stakeholders underlying emotions and motivations in exchange for their Investments, Purchases, Loyalty, and Trust.

This Strategy Alignment capability must be measured and monitored for Value-Realization through Best-In-Class Data Management Operations and Support, Information-Value Governance, and Continuous Learning and Development cycles that deliver expected outcomes and impacts. **Figure 6** depicts a visualization of the Information Management Engine Model.

In summary, these core elements: stakeholder emotive, strategy enablement capability, information value realization measurement, monitoring, and management for expected outcomes and impacts are all wrapped in a culture of best practices for pivotal Information and Technology management trade practices. Precisely, Business Analysis, Project Management, Solution Architecture, Solution Development, and Human Resource Management & Administration form the driving force for delivering primary stakeholder perceived information value. As a result, the Information Management Engine begins with Stakeholder Value Emotive.

Embrace Stakeholder Value Motives

Primary Stakeholders

A *stakeholder* is a person or group of people who own a share in a business or who have an interest in its success.[35] In business information and technology management, a stakeholder is any person, group, organization, or entity affected by a project, product, service, or experience resulting from an investment, purchase, or exchange of time, money, or expertise for something of equal or more excellent value.

Many stakeholder personas are mentioned in modern business literature, notably *business owners, investors, customers,* and *employees*. For purposes of this work, I refer to these as primary stakeholders to differentiate them from all other stakeholders because of the outsized role they play in the success or failure of an organization to meet its particular Business Ultimatum.

The emotions and motivations coming from these personas often create and drive entire industries, disruptive innovations, and high levels of achievement. Think briefly about the passion and drive exemplified by the great artisans of the ancient world, modern industry leaders, scientific visionaries, and inventors whose accomplishments we enjoy and use daily: electric light, trains, automobiles, ships, airplanes, vaccines and medicines, satellites, spacecraft, and many more. All trace their origins to the emotions and motivations

---

[35] Cambridge Dictionary, s.v. "Stakeholder," accessed March 6, 2023, https://dictionary.cambridge.org/dictionary/english/stakeholder.

of one or more primary stakeholders.

What motivates them? What emotions drive them day in and day out? Why do they persevere through trial and tribulation, "through thick and thin"? And perhaps most importantly, what do they value most? What are they willing to exchange for the things they love most, and how do they perceive and measure the realization of the things they're ready to trade for them? What impacts those around them as they pursue fulfillment and gratification, to scratch the passions that itch in exchange for the things they value most? All these questions are at the heart of primary stakeholder *value motives* and *emotions*.

Here are some examples of value motives for different business stakeholders:

1. **Customers** -
    - High-quality products or services that meet their needs and expectations
    - Competitive pricing and value for their money
    - Excellent customer service and support
    - Convenience and ease of use in their interactions with the business
    - Trust and reliability in the products or services offered

2. **Investors** -
    - Strong financial returns and profitability
    - Growth potential and capital appreciation
    - Risk mitigation and protection of their investment
    - Transparent and ethical business practices
    - Long-term sustainability and a positive reputation in the market

3. **Employees** -
    - Fair compensation and benefits

- Opportunities for career growth and development
- Work-life balance and a supportive work environment
- Recognition and appreciation for their contributions
- Job security and stability

4. **Suppliers** -
   - Timely payments and fair business practices
   - Long-term partnerships and collaboration opportunities
   - Clear communication and efficient supply chain management
   - Mutual growth and success through a strong business relationship

5. **Communities** -
   - Social responsibility and contributions to local development
   - Environmental sustainability and responsible resource management
   - Job creation and economic impact
   - Collaboration and engagement with community initiatives
   - Enhancing the overall quality of life in the community

In a business context, emotions can be influenced by an inspirational marketing campaign, compelling product branding message, exciting new product design rollout, or other activity that seeks to engage customers, employees, or stakeholders through their feelings. The goal is to drive a stronger connection between the business and its customers, employees, or investors, which can lead to greater brand loyalty, improved access to capital, and greater employee retention.

An organization's primary stakeholders make

important decisions about when, where, and with whom to exchange their valuable time and money. For instance, investors decide which businesses or organizations give them the most significant returns in exchange for their financial resources. If their strong emotions and motivations for doing so are unmet, they have the prerogative to shift their valuable resources to opportunities for a better return on investment.

Similarly, customers exchange their loyalty, advocacy, and trust in businesses that give them an equal or greater value in return; otherwise, they take their business elsewhere, and the offending organization suffers losses in revenue, and sales, higher employee turnover and other forms of increased costs. Metrics like customer loyalty scores, product defects, return rates, and, most recently, the net promoter score[36] provide a means of determining whether the business is delivering customer-perceived value.

Information and technology management professionals must realize that powerful emotions and motivations drive human behavior in many different environmental contexts, situations, personas, or circumstances, including individual contributors, middle- and senior-level managers, contractors, customers, vendors, and peers. Each stakeholder plays a role in an organization's ability to deliver information value.

Seasoned ITM professionals recognize and act on these emotions and motivations with skill and foresight. Who are the new digital transformation project proponents and the detractors and

---

[36] Net Promoter Score (NPS) is calculated by subtracting the percentage of detractors from the percentage of promoters. This helps businesses determine how well they create active product and service advocates.

contrarians? How much power and influence do they have, and what information is needed to persuade them? Are they persuadable, or will they remain entrenched against the initiative and require a different approach?

Stakeholder Emotions and Motivations

Demand-side stakeholders' emotions and motivations can range from simple (such as the fear of failure) to complex (such as innate desire to win or passion for service) in the same person. The critical point is that these emotions and motivations influence customers' purchase decisions or investors' release of capital.

Sales and marketing professionals seek such insights from market information or business intelligence. Financial planning and analysis professionals seek capital markets and investors. Therefore, supply-side stakeholders such as information and Technology Management professionals, provide essential capabilities to research and discover these insights for sales, marketing, and financial planning and analysis clients.

Table 5 depicts the alignment between some important stakeholder emotional motivations and an organization's business focus areas. I'm sure you can think of additional examples to explain why customers choose certain brands over others, why investors choose certain businesses over others, and why employees choose to work for certain companies over others.

Table 5. Business Stakeholder Emotions and Needs

Business focus areas	Emotional motivation	Stakeholder motivation

Embrace Stakeholder Value Motive

Business Ultimatum	Need to survive and grow	Strong will to succeed
Value delivery	Desire to help others	Powerful passion for service
Goal accomplishment	Desire for completion	Deep desire to achieve
Market leadership	Desire to be the best	Relentless pursuit of excellence
Research& development	Desire to create	Hunger to innovate & invent
Market leadership	Desire for competition	A profound desire to win
Goal accomplishment	Desire for contentment	Relentless pursuit of happiness
Business communication	Need for self-expression	Passion for being heard & understood

Chapter Summary

Having a thorough understanding of the emotions and motivations of key stakeholders is crucial for senior leaders. This understanding enables them to align strategic goals and effectively allocate available resources to deliver measurable, scalable, and sustainable value, as defined by these stakeholders. As a result, the practice of efficiently cascading goals throughout the organization becomes essential in tackling the challenges of the Business Ultimatum.

Motivate Strategic Alignment

Strategy Lifecycle Management is the art and science of enabling the optimal approach to achieve an organization's mission, vision, purpose, and values within a given set of constraints, notably time, talent, competition, regulatory obligations, and available capital. Strategic alignment helps to determine the chief challenges, hurdles, and obstacles an organization must overcome to meet its Business Ultimatum. As a result, it is a significant responsibility of business owners, boards of directors, headquarters, and leadership at all levels to ensure the most effective and efficient strategies, programs, processes, policies and standards cascade throughout the organization. As a result, one of their most important objectives is to align process and technology implementation, adoption, execution, measurement, and continuous improvement with the organization's strategies to deliver primary stakeholder perceived value realization and desired experiences.

Therefore, strategic alignment is a crucial state that emerges from the dedicated efforts of strong leadership at all levels of the organization. These leaders are committed to efficiently and effectively deploying the company's skilled trade practitioners, strategists, and tacticians, who act as the organization's "special forces." They are motivated to bring the company's mission, vision, values, and strategic priorities to fruition.

These leaders ensure that the organization's strategies are deeply ingrained throughout the company. This is achieved through cascading goals, objectives, metrics, and key performance indicators that are tailored to each team, department, and individual personnel involved. By doing so, they ensure that the organization's values and priorities are consistently reflected in meaningful ways that are appropriate to the specific contexts and roles within the organization.

To achieve strategic alignment, information management personnel must work closely with their senior leaders to assess current solution performance against best practice standards and the capabilities required to meet the moment. They convert SMART questions into computer queries, dashboards, reports, and visualizations that answer probes such as:

1. Are the company's strategies aligned with its overall goals and objectives?
2. How well do the strategies address the needs and expectations of the target market?
3. What measurable outcomes and results have been achieved as a result of implementing the strategies?
4. Are the strategies adaptable and responsive to changes in the business environment?
5. How well do employees understand and support the strategies, and do they have the necessary resources and capabilities to execute them effectively?

These questions focus on the alignment of strategies with goals, the impact on target market, the achievement of measurable results, the flexibility to adapt, and the employee's understanding and support of the strategies. They provide key insights into the effectiveness and success of the company's strategic initiatives.

The basic mechanism for aligning an organization's primary assets is to empower and execute the *strategy management lifecycle* process, which entails four major phases.

- Strategy analysis and formulation

- Strategy deployment and adoption

- Strategy measurement and monitoring

- Continuous improvement-change management

These elements are how inspirational leaders identify and choose the best strategic options in moments that matter most over a sustained period.

Strategy Analysis and Formulation

The analysis and formulation of strategies begin with an organization's commitment to its mission, vision, values, and purpose. These elements serve as the emotional driving force behind the desires and ambitions of the organization's leaders. Through strategy analysis and formulation, the organization determines the most effective methods and approaches to achieve its goals and objectives and deliver value to stakeholders. This process also sets priorities, manages performance, handles projects and processes, manages risks, makes decisions, solves problems, and converts opportunities.

As a result, this process relies on the input, processing, and output of data, which transforms into valuable insights. Information management engineers play a critical role in analyzing, defining, and designing the data solutions required for managing the strategy lifecycle. They collaborate with senior leadership strategists to develop powerful management tools such as Balanced Scorecards and Strategy Maps. These tools help analyze and evaluate the performance of various processes, programs, and portfolios that are essential to the organization's success.

Balanced scorecards and strategy maps were pioneered by author and educator Robert S. Kaplan and David P. Norton, business theorist and consultant. Both senior executives, they highlight the criticality and opportunities to achieve strategic alignment in their books *The Balanced Scorecard: Translating Strategy into Action* and *The Strategy Focused Organization: How Balanced Scorecard Companies Thrive in the New Business Environment*.

Kaplan and Norton define a balanced scorecard as a "set of measures that gives top managers a fast, comprehensive view of the business. The balanced scorecard includes financial measures that show the actions taken." [37] According to Koch (2003), a company's strategy is *"a model of how an organization creates value. Strategy is how you intend to create value for your shareholders"* (para. 5). And Kaplan (as cited in Koch, 2003) advised IT executives to *"define the strategy, participate in this process. Then everybody has a way to align their activities to the strategy. Everyone is then strategic"* (para. 14). [38]

Balance scorecards and strategy maps are excellent frameworks for strategy analysis and formulation. Similarly, the objectives and key results (OKR) framework are ideal for deriving high-priority objectives, goals, and expected outcomes via accurate cause-and-effect decision-making based on techniques like statistical correlation analysis, scatter plots,

---

[37] Kaplan, R. S., & Norton, D. P. (1992). The balanced scorecard--Measures that drive performance. Harvard Business Review, 70(1), 71-79.

[38] Koch, C. (2003). The real business value of IT. CIO Magazine. Retrieved from https://www.cio.com/article/2441977/the-real-business-value-of-it.html

and other tools.[39] Most organizations that deploy balanced scorecards and OKR frameworks adapt them to their organization's culture and processes to help improve effectiveness, deployment, and adoption. The dataflows into and out of these frameworks are essential elements of information management engineering.

Think about the input data, information, and insight necessary to develop a balanced scorecard, accurately answer strategic questions, and derive the most effective-efficient Strategic Roadmap to accomplish the organization's primary purpose. Dwell on the people, technology, and professional practices required to ensure that all the inputs to balanced scorecards and strategy maps are thorough, accurate, complete, relevant, and timely. information management engineers, like business analysts, solution architects, and process engineers, are responsible for this assurance. They leverage analytical tools, technologies, and techniques such as:

- Predictive analysis (What will most likely happen?),

- Descriptive analysis (What happened?),

- Diagnostic analysis (Why did it happen?)

- Prescriptive analysis (What is the next best action?)

- Root Cause analysis (Why did it happen?)

---

[39] White, S. K. (2018, September 4). What is OKR? A goal-setting framework for thinking. CIO Magazine. Retrieved from https://www.cio.com/article/3213590/what-is-okr-a-goal-setting-framework-for-thinking-big.html

- SWOT analysis (What are our strengths, weaknesses, opportunities, and threats?)

In addition, data security analysts, data governance officers, and data quality engineers ensure these analyses are based on secure, accurate, timely, complete, and relevant data. They create and maintain metadata (data about data)[40] catalogs that link frequently asked business-critical questions to solution dashboards and visualizations through a lineage of discovery that is easy to access and puts answers at the fingertips of key decision-makers. High-quality data and insight are a primary need of any organization operating in the digital age of information management.

Then the information management engineers analyze those performance results for input data, knowledge, and business intelligence into the strategy formulation effort. They help to determine critical constraints and requirements for budget, human talent, and technology considerations. They dig deep into market research, customer experience scores, and business partner performance to determine potential impacts on strategy formulation and decision-making. High-quality information, business intelligence, and decision-making are the critical outcomes of strategy analysis and formulation.

Because continuously improving business information management enables firms to ask better strategic questions that lead to intelligent investments in the capability to perform. As described earlier, better business questions lead to specific, relevant,

---

[40] Metadata is "data about data." It documents and supports key definitions for specific databases, tables, columns, and reports. Metadata includes things like data dictionaries, business glossary of data terms, metrics libraries and report catalogs.

significant, and intuitive insights that drive actionable business intelligence. The more primary stakeholders trust their information, the more precise their questions become and the fewer assumptions they make. This helps reduce uncertainty and lower risks during strategy analysis and formulation.

In their book **The Value Factor**: *How Global Leaders Use Information for Growth and Competitive Advantage,* Mark Hurd and Lars Nyberg highlight the findings of Kim Collins, a leading analyst with Gartner Inc. She points out that a company must track at least seven critical categories that require high-quality information to manage: customer satisfaction, economics, market share, customer loyalty, customer profitability, marketing campaigns, and market metrics.[41]

Measuring business operations is critical to success; the value of metrics like those Collins listed depends on the quality of the business's questions and the availability of high-quality information. *"The number one risk factor in any organization is lack of accurate information"* (Hurd & Nyberg, 2004).

The main goal of strategy analysis and formulation is to ensure that the organization's strategic plans and decisions are comprehensive, focused, and responsive to the current needs. This desired outcome depends on the effective utilization of talent, technologies, processes, and information management practices to establish sustainable strategic alignment.

---

[41] Hurd, M., & Nyberg, B. (2004). The value factor: How global leaders use information for growth and competitive advantage. New York, NY: McGraw-Hill.pg. 62,63

Motivate Strategic Alignment

Strategy Deployment and Adoption

Strategy deployment and adoption represent the implementation stage of the strategy lifecycle management. The goal is to translate the efforts invested in strategy analysis and formulation into practical action plans that cascade throughout the organization. These action plans are designed to align with the underlying motivations of primary stakeholders and the organization's mission, vision, and values.

To achieve this, information management practitioners need to have a thorough understanding of their trade and utilize established tools and techniques. This ensures that the selected strategies are effectively deployed throughout the organization through efficient goal cascades. It is crucial for these strategies to be embraced by key stakeholders, capturing their hearts and minds.

Implementing successful strategies requires business intelligence, which emphasizes the importance of information management engineers. These professionals must utilize their personal interaction skills, including genuine empathy towards stakeholder concerns, recognizing and acknowledging primary stakeholder motivations, actively listening to gain deeper understanding, and demonstrating enthusiasm in serving the organization's strategic goals.

First and foremost, strategy deployment involves the intentional implementation of the organization's chosen methods of delivering value in its sponsored projects, programs, processes, and portfolios. These four elements play a vital role in enabling the organization to achieve the ultimate purpose of strategy deployment and adoption. In addition, activities, incentives, rewards, and recognition serve as important drivers in promoting the successful adoption and implementation of the organization's strategies.

The objective is to ensure action plans have direct linkage and continuous, bi-directional feedback from strategic priorities into the performance goals and incentives of the executive board, senior leadership, directors, managers (especially people managers) to individual contributors, and especially pivotal professional trade-practitioners employing information management engineering concepts. Consider the underlying data, calculations, and computations that inform decisions about which actions will yield the most profitable results. Think about processing marketing campaign data, sentiment analysis data, academic research, technology innovations, and social media data into helpful business intelligence-based decision-making and problem-solving activities.

Therefore, strategy deployment emphasizes identifying, harmonizing, and developing project plans, roadmaps, and processes most appropriate for specific teams and individuals in cascading order. People managers, business process architects, and business analysts need access to health information management systems to design and deliver high project success rates, resilient program effectiveness, and sustainable process efficiencies.

There are several approaches and frameworks for strategy deployment, and undoubtedly more to come. One of my favorites is Hoshin Kanri: the *catch-ball*. I like the simplicity of this analogy because it implies one "ball" or strategy that all players must receive, respect, acknowledge, execute, iterate, and interact within the expectations and norms of their roles and pass back and forth where appropriate.

To expand the analogy into sports like basketball, consider the information needed to formulate a strategic game plan and playbook designed to win the championship. The strategy ball flows from personnel managers and head coaches to position coaches and team leaders to the rest of the team. The team executes the game plan with constant real-time feedback to team leaders and coaches. Then, the team conducts post-game analysis using film from specific plays, situations, and competitor reactions. These ultimately lead to adjustments in the strategy playbook, insight into talent requirements, and team performance. In this sense, everyone is responsible for advancing the ball and scoring. Business organizations that follow Hoshin Kanri's approach share a similar dynamic to sports analogies of strategy playbook analysis, formulation, deployment to the team, player execution, and bidirectional feedback loops between players, coaches, managers, and owners.

Again, information management personnel are pivotal to ensuring that each succeeding and preceding level of the organization has access to the necessary information to make this framework effective and efficient. For instance, data management engineers, data architects, and data scientists enable business information solutions, artificial intelligence, and advanced analytics to correlate game-time decisions to real-time results. Results analysis ultimately drives the iterative energy cycles of feedback up and down the organization.

The core aim of strategy deployment is to achieve the highest return on investment in strategy analysis and formulation. Methods like Hoshin Kanri help to ensure that this investment is monitored, managed, executed, and measured from end-to-end, from the most senior executive to every individual contributor. Annual meetings, quarterly webinars, organizational change management initiatives, communication campaigns, frequent manager-to-employee one-to-one reviews, and action plans contribute to strategy deployment effectiveness.

Once the strategy has been deployed, it is essential for it to be adopted, embraced, and integrated throughout the organization. This adoption should be evident in every team's charter, purpose statement, goals, objectives, incentives, and performance measures. To adopt a strategy means to fully embrace it, value it, and recognize its importance.

Strategy adoption is arguably the most crucial aspect of the strategy management lifecycle. It measures the organization's ability to align its technology investments, processes, and production efficiencies with the attitudes, behaviors, and emotional energy of key enablers. When employees at all levels of the organization are highly motivated and empowered with clear strategic direction, along with the right technologies, tools, processes, and emotional support, they have the best chance of achieving success.

Accumulating and retaining top talent, expertise, experience, and effective emotional leadership is one of the ways an organization improves strategy adoption. The idea is to find, advocate and encourage those attitudes and behaviors that recognize and respect the Business Ultimatum, then promote, incentivize, and appeal to their intrinsic desire to achieve. Such organizations that implement Human resource management applications like PeopleSoft, Workday, or other HRMS coupled with IT service management solutions like ServiceNow, SAP, or Atlassian empower HR IT managers, HR specialists, and business managers to build resilient organization change management frameworks that support strong strategy adoption campaigns to yield persistent strategic alignment conditions.

Some essential activities of effective strategy adoption are townhall sessions, webinars and conferences, periodic business result updates, and ongoing recognition programs for teams and individuals that consistently demonstrate expected business outcomes. Monetary awards, bonuses, and merit increases are powerful motivators of the desired behavior; however, cultivating a spirit of belonging, inclusion, and team recognition are also significant incentives measured through employee satisfaction metrics and measures.

Senior business analysts, process managers, solution architects, and data scientists work closely with internal change agents and thought leaders to establish meaningful measures of leading and lagging indicators that provide essential insight to primary decision authorities. The information necessary to enable accurate, meaningful strategy measurement and monitoring include data regarding internal and external signals, such as customer sentiments, experiences, and expectations; employee focus, productivity, and enthusiasm; process efficiencies and innovation.

Strategy Measurement and Monitoring

Strategy measurement and monitoring is the "prove it" phase of strategy lifecycle management. It includes evaluating the effectiveness of information management solutions and technology investments to enable key process capabilities, better forecast accuracies, root-level problem resolution, differential innovations, and reliable regulatory compliance.

Information management engineers help to design and develop strategic scorecards, dashboards, and reports that directly answer the best measurement questions and provide strategic alerts when the strategy veers from the control threshold. These professionals help deploy applications like Tableau, PowerBI, Google Analytics, Amazon Web Services, and other technologies per the actual, underlying business requirements and needs for valuable answers.

Typically, such technologies enable high-level executive summaries that provide insight at a glance and drill-down features to allow analysts to seek an in-depth understanding and explanation of the state of the organization's objectives and key results. Accurate strategic alignment up and down the organization is challenging without these capabilities to measure, monitor, and improve strategic decision-making.

As described earlier, the balanced scorecard, objectives, key results, and other frameworks are predicated on the ability and capacity to capture, store, transform, analyze, and cascade relevant, accurate, timely data into meaningful insight tailored to each business unit, function, department, team, and individual that it is intended to enable. Then, these informed insights are transformed into more efficient feedback loops between senior leaders and their strategists, facilitated by relevant IM trade practitioners for better decision-making, improved internal consulting, and greater fulfillment of primary stakeholder needs in response to the Business Ultimatum for strategic alignment.

Strategic performance measurement and monitoring are most effective in quantitative and qualitative terms. Quantitative measures such as those found in the financial statements like the balance sheet, income statement, and cash flow statements like financial ratios of price-to-earnings, earnings-per-share, or debt-to-equity are necessary to evaluate the effectiveness of the organization's strategy. Key measures such as the formula to calculate economic valued added quantify value creation from a financial perspective. [42]

Qualitative measures help evaluate primary stakeholders' experiences, sentiments, preferences, and emotional reactions. The net promoter score (NPS) is an example of a qualitative measure. It is widely used in market research to measure the likelihood that a customer would recommend a company, a product, or a service to people in their network. NPS organizes respondents into three categories on a scale of numeric ranges: a "Detractor" rates at six or below, a "Passive" respondent rates 7 or 8, and a "Promoter" rates 9 or 10 on the scale. Net promoter score is considered a measure of customer loyalty.

In addition to NPS, traditional measures such as employee satisfaction, customer satisfaction, or preferred supplier surveys, interviews, and observational experiences provide instrumental analysis. Business owners, senior leaders, and managers do well to prioritize qualitative measures for their pivotal information management engineering functions. Especially given the pace of digitization in the competitive landscape, an organization's competitive edge can be traced to the health of its project management, business analysis, solution architecture, process engineering, solution development, and support. These critical trade practices enable strategic change management and

---

[42] EVA = NOPAT − (total assets - current liabilities) * WACC

continuous improvement cycles.

Continual Improvement - Change Management

Continual improvement is the practice of incremental, step-by-step pursuit of better and better inputs and transformation of those inputs to improved outputs that better serve the primary stakeholder's physical, financial, and emotional needs. From an information service management perspective of strategic alignment, the Information Technology Infrastructure Library® (ITIL®) framework provides a robust roadmap for organizations to pursue continual improvement.

Professional IM trade practitioners leverage their training in the seven-step continual service improvement process defined by ITIL to help achieve the underlying intent of sustainable progress. These seven improvement milestones informed by ITILv3 answer the questions "What should you measure?" and "What can you measure?", then gather, process, and analyze the measurement data. Next, "Present and use the information" and "take corrective actions" to realize the improvement. Again, well-trained and supported information management engineers consistently bring these core competencies to organizations willing to support and invest in them.

Continual improvement in any competitive landscape is essential to addressing the Business Ultimatum. Organizations that embrace this practice, as its underlying commitment to deliver information value realization, must continually turn to the most effective tools, techniques, and talents available to manage the changes continual improvement necessitate.

Change management is essential to sustaining strategic alignment of the organizations' capabilities to continually improve value delivery and meet its Business Ultimatum. First, organizations must have an inherent acknowledgment that change is a constant factor — if for no other reason because of the natural lifecycle of things, which influences and impacts customer, investor, and employee experiences and motivations.

Consequently, information management professionals must be attentive to change impacts of every kind, including technological, environmental, process, and mainly organizational. Organizational change management (OCM) is the discipline of communicating, coordinating, and controlling planned and unplanned change factors impacting people in the organization and their capabilities to perform critical tasks. This is often a significant focus of human resource management professionals and people managers across the organization. Some organizations specifically create OCM teams to steward the organization through large-scale transformations and change events.

Change itself can be a significant emotional challenge for an organization and its personnel due to the idea of a "comfort zone" for things we're familiar with or have come to expect. However, continuous improvement implies constantly pursuing "change for the better." As a result, change leaders must pay attention to the psychological impact of change on the organization's cultural norms, practices, language, and behaviors. To this end, the effects of change on people, processes, and technologies must be diligently observed, forecasted, analyzed, measured, and managed by accountable executives and direct line managers.

Such as change impacts resulting from internal turnover or attrition of subject matter experts or the introduction of new technologies, changes in environmental regulations, or changes in the strength of primary competitors. Change itself necessitates vigilant measuring, monitoring, and evaluating the potency of the organization's strategy due to several change drivers.

Michael E. Porter's 1979 Five Forces Model describes a set of significant drivers underlying the profitability and attractiveness of an organization's industry.[43] Porter describes five change drivers that influence an organization's ability to compete within their industries:

1) **The bargaining power of its suppliers.**
   Industries with more suppliers tend to increase competition and lower the prices suppliers charge businesses due to the laws of supply and demand. The greater the supply, the lower the costs; conversely, the lower the supply, the higher the prices suppliers can charge.

2) **The threat of new entrants into the market.**
   Industries with lower barriers to entry tend to invite new entrants, which can lead to lower market share for any given company. The more competitors in a given market, the more the market is split between those with staying power.

3) **The threat of substitute products or services.**
   Industries with products that are readily copied, substituted, or replaced by other brands tend to increase competition and lower prices. This is very beneficial to consumers because it gives them more choices and more reasonable prices. Generic brands illustrate this point compared to name-brand products,

---

[43] Porter, M. E. (1980). Competitive strategy: Techniques for analyzing industries and competitors. New York, NY: The Free Press.

such as the case with products like antifreeze, toothpaste, laundry detergents, and many others. Conversely, unique products and services can command higher prices, margins, and market share. Examples of unique products, such as rare earth metals, in specific industries illustrate this point.

4) **The bargaining power of its customers/buyers.** The exercise of choice by consumers and investors, as measured by their brand loyalty, net promoter scores, and willingness to invest, tends towards lower prices, margins, and market share for products and services that are readily available. All commercial organizations are directly influenced by this competitive force to one degree or another and must pay careful attention to the wants, needs, and experiences of their customers and investors relative to competitors.

5) **Industry rivalry.** Companies that operate in industries with strong, direct competition are greatly influenced by decisions that impact the prices they can charge, the amount they spend on advertising and marketing, the size of their workforce, and their capabilities to comply with applicable laws and regulations.

The direct effect of any of these change drivers or the cumulative impact of these industry change drivers necessitates professional information management core products and services. Notably, business analysts and data governance managers help track these changes' impact on the organization's most critical business data elements by using data lineage-metadata management tools, business, and technical requirements traceability techniques, data modeling, process modeling, and data flow diagram libraries-of-record. Data scientists and external consultants help to define the input parameters and source information for advanced analytics models to help simulate change impacts.

In addition, project and organizational change managers charter, organize, communicate, and control project initiatives to manage the internal change impacts of the five forces across the organization. They help answer questions like; what is the effect of the five forces on our IT infrastructure? What is the impact of the five forces on our marketing strategy? What is the result of the five forces on our sales priorities? How do these five forces impact our core competencies and talent management strategy? How does the organization marshal its capabilities to perform in a manner that to the positive side of the financial statements?

In addition to the Five Forces Model, Michael Porter developed the powerful practice of *value chain management* as a practical approach to designing and delivering value realization. A value chain is a series of strategically aligned process-oriented activities optimized to deliver perceptible, measurable value to customers and investors.

Strategically aligning all information technology and process management capabilities for continual improvement of the organization's value-delivery engine is critically important to investors, senior leadership, and all people managers. Specifically, this supports critical enablers like business analysts, process engineers, and project managers who must effectively collaborate with solution architects, business strategists, external consultants, and others to design, develop, execute, measure, and continually improve strategic alignment of the value-deliver chain to company goals and priorities.

Chapter Summary

The Strategy Management Lifecycle aligns an organization's essential assets, including information assets, to achieve its primary goals and objectives. The core phases of the strategy alignment lifecycle include strategy analysis and formulation, strategy deployment and adoption, strategy measurement and monitoring, and continual improvement-change management.

Strategy analysis and formulation start with an organization's fidelity to its mission, vision, values, and purpose. It is the emotional fuel behind the principals' desires and ambitions. Analyzing and forming strategies determines the best methods and means by which an organization's goals and objectives will be realized and stakeholder value delivered.

Strategy deployment and adoption is the execution phase of strategy lifecycle management. Its purpose is to transform the investment in strategy analysis and formulation into cascading, cause-and-effect action plans aligned to the primary stakeholders' underlying motivations and the organization's mission, vision, and values.

Strategy measurement and monitoring is the "prove it" phase of strategy lifecycle management. It includes evaluating the effectiveness of information management solutions and technology investments to enable key process capabilities, better forecast accuracies, root-level problem resolution, differential innovations, and reliable regulatory compliance.

Continual improvement is the practice of

incremental, step-by-step pursuit of better and better inputs and transformation of those inputs to improved outputs that better serve the primary stakeholder's physical, financial, and emotional needs.

change management is essential to sustaining strategic alignment of the organizations' capabilities to improve value delivery and meet its Business Ultimatum continually. Change is a constant factor due to the natural lifecycle of things, influencing and causing impacts on the customer, investor, and employee experiences and motivations.

Effective information managers and engineers anticipate, predict, and game out potential change impacts as a function of day-to-day business intelligence operations and thought processes. They inherently recognize and acknowledge that change is an inevitable outcome of the lifecycle-of-things and that those with the capabilities to maximize their strengths and opportunities while minimizing the effects of their weaknesses and threats sustain their organization's strategic alignment to primary stakeholder value-delivery. Two critical lifecycles that merit high-performance information management engineering are the requirements management and solutions management lifecycle.

PART III: Manage Critical Information Lifecycles

Everything in the world has a lifecycle. This means that everything we love, cherish, and value goes through a cycle of existence. Whether it's something we buy, build, touch, see, hear, or smell, it follows a natural law that governs its beginning, middle, and end. This principle of nature is evident in various stages like inception, birth, growth, maturity, decline, and expiration. We often refer to this concept as "The Circle of Life."

It's important to note that this lifecycle principle applies to both living and non-living things. Let's take stars as an example. Stars are formed when huge clouds of dust collapse under gravity. They go through phases of growth, maturity, decline, and eventually collapse over millions of years. As they collapse, they release chemical elements that become part of new lifecycles throughout the universe. These elements form planets, living organism like humans, plants, animals and even human-made products.

Most importantly, a living thing's life cycle suggests an urgency to maximize its optimal productivity stages, specifically growth and maturity. In other words, the ultimatum is to produce while productive. The cutoff period starts when something begins to decline and continues until it becomes obsolete or expires. Therefore, in order to achieve the highest level of productivity during the growth and maturity phase, it is crucial to have access to relevant, timely, and accurate information.

The Information Management Engine

This information helps us locate and process the necessary inputs to achieve our desired outcomes: survival and growth. As we discussed before, this is the intended function of the natural senses in living organisms.

Applying the highest level of investment attention to information lifecycle management is imperative because business transaction data requirements are the starting point of the organization's value chain delivery to customers and investors. Take a moment to reflect on the real meaning of the word "requirement." It refers to something that needs to be done in order for something else to occur. It could be a demand, a legal obligation, or a condition that must be met. You can think of it as synonymous with critical needs, must-haves, requisites, or a state of necessity.

In this regard, Thomas Maslow's hierarchy of needs can be applied to a business organization to help highlight significant differences between "must-haves" and "nice-to-have." A need is a condition of necessity; for instance, an organization must have sufficient operating capital, technology, employees, and customers to meet its business ultimatum. Some organizations refer to must-haves as a minimum viable product (MVP). Versus nice-to-haves like an on-site recreational room for employees, a daycare center for parents, or quarterly bonuses even during an economic downturn.

That's why the natural law that governs the lifecycle of things is crucial for the Information Management Engine and plays a key role in understanding the significance of data, information, and insight. The unchanging nature embedded in the lifecycle of things turns our instinctual drive for survival into the emotional energy necessary to translate essential data requirements into informed actions with clear cause-and-effect relationships. It helps us establish a balance between the amount of information we have and the actions we take based on that information.

Consequently, organizations should take this lesson from natural laws to highlight the criticality of managing the most consequential lifecycles within their span of control and influence. To this end, the purpose of the following three chapters is to emphasize some of the most consequential lifecycles of any modern company operating in the digital age of business.

Specifically, the information lifecycle, requirements lifecycle management, and solution lifecycle management. These three lifecycles profoundly affect the organization's subsequent product and service lifecycles, which are vital in the customer value delivery train.

Assure Business Information Lifecycle Management

Information and data serve as the vital lifeblood of every modern business organization. They are essential for conducting and managing business operations effectively. In particular, business and financial transaction data circulate throughout the organization in diverse forms, ranging from detailed records to summarized and transformed information. The Information Management Engine recognizes the significance of the information lifecycle and views it as a collaborative effort involving key IM trade practices and their stakeholders.

To ensure the smooth flow and optimal utilization of information, it is crucial to initiate the information lifecycle with well-planned and prescheduled capacity planning cycles. This involves anticipating the organization's future data needs, assessing current and projected data volumes, and aligning the necessary resources to accommodate the expected data growth. Simultaneously, upfront data quality control planning is essential. This entails establishing rigorous processes and protocols for ensuring the accuracy, integrity, and reliability of data from the outset.

Implementation of the data quality control plan is then carried out, involving the adoption of standardized data collection methods, utilization of data cleansing and validation techniques, and implementing appropriate data governance practices. Once implemented, continuous measurement and monitoring of data quality become integral components of the information lifecycle. Regular assessments and audits help identify areas for improvement, ensure adherence to data quality standards, and allow for timely corrective actions when deviations are detected.

By emphasizing the importance of capacity planning and data quality control from the onset, organizations can establish a strong foundation for effective information management. This proactive approach enables businesses to leverage high-quality data for decision-making, improve operational efficiency, enhance customer experiences, and drive overall organizational success.

Capacity Planning and Data Quality Control Points

The management of the business information lifecycle begins with comprehensive planning to effectively capture, store, utilize, retain, archive, and eventually obsolete business and financial transaction data. This process involves close collaboration between various professionals such as data engineers, database administrators, enterprise architects, business analysts, project managers, and data scientists.

The goal is to forecast the volume and nature of input data generated by business activities, which then flows into computer applications, databases, data factories, data lakes, and data warehouses. These professionals work together to ensure that the organization has sufficient computing resources, including CPU, memory, communications, and storage capacity, to handle the processing requirements of sales orders, invoices, inventory management, shipping and receiving, payments, purchase orders, customer service cases, as well as the maintenance of financial journals, ledgers, and statements in compliance with relevant regulations.

Considering that business volumes can vary in cycles, be influenced by seasonal patterns, or remain relatively stable, information management (IM) professionals must employ tactics and techniques to accommodate each of these possibilities. They need to anticipate fluctuations in data volume and implement strategies to handle peak periods efficiently without sacrificing performance or data quality. This may involve scaling computing resources, optimizing data storage and retrieval processes, and utilizing parallel processing techniques to handle increased workloads.

Furthermore, IM professionals must ensure regulatory compliance throughout the information lifecycle. This entails adhering to data retention policies, safeguarding sensitive information, and facilitating audits and regulatory reporting as required by industry standards or legal requirements.

By employing proactive planning, collaboration, and adaptable strategies, organizations can effectively manage the business information lifecycle. This allows them to process and utilize data efficiently, maintain accurate and reliable records, comply with regulations, and make informed business decisions based on the insights derived from their data assets.

In some cases, cloud-computing technology is most appropriate, mainly when the need for computing power is somewhat elastic; it can go down at any given time. In addition, large volumes of unstructured data, such as photos, audio, and video, demand large amounts of storage and processing capacity, which may help determine the most appropriate capacity plan to meet that need.

In some situations, a business may determine that having computing power on-site or on-premises is the most suitable option for their requirements. This could be the case for companies operating in countries with strict data security compliance regulations. These regulations may mandate that data must be stored and processed within a specific geographical location. Additionally, businesses that deal with highly sensitive or proprietary formulas may prefer to have on-premises computing power. Information Technology Management (ITM) professionals need to take all these factors into account and plan accordingly during the initial stages of the information lifecycle.

It is important to note that computer capacity planning and forecasting is a nuanced process, much like financial planning and forecasting. It involves a combination of data science, predictive statistical analysis, and the expertise and experience of enterprise architects and specialists in their respective fields. Some aspects require the unique skills and specialized knowledge that can only be acquired through practice and time. You may have encountered someone in your own work experiences who fits this description.

By recognizing the complexity and importance of these considerations, organizations can ensure they make informed decisions regarding their computing power and effectively plan for their future information management needs.

The business information lifecycle should consider data quality and security control at various points. This means identifying the steps in the business workflow process where it's best to apply quality and security control measures. Ideally, these controls should be implemented as early as possible in the process cycle to ensure effectiveness without causing unnecessary disruptions or hindering efficiency and productivity. It is crucial for process engineers to closely collaborate with data architects to strike a balance between risk management and maintaining an optimal flow rate for delivering value.

In the design of the process, engineering should highlight these control points within the value delivery train. This can be achieved by integrating important business process workflow diagrams with relevant data flow diagrams and appropriately labeling data quality and security checkpoints. For instance, planning and documenting data entry edit-checks and using appropriate notation for business and data rules should be done based on the level of risk involved. Additionally, points of data access security permission should be designed and emphasized.

By incorporating these considerations into the business information lifecycle, organizations can enhance data quality, ensure security, and manage risks effectively. This enables a smooth and secure flow of information, ensuring that critical data is protected while maintaining the efficiency and productivity necessary for value delivery.

To ensure the accuracy and usefulness of business data, it is important to plan for additional data quality control points during the process of transferring data to downstream data repositories. This helps establish a seamless flow of reliable information from the source to the target systems, as well as to all recipients downstream. The purpose of implementing these control points is to maintain a consistent and trustworthy "one-version-of-truth" for the business data and ensure that it is suitable and reliable for its intended purposes.

Assure Business Information Lifecycle Management

Data Capture, Storage, and Access Management

Like everything else, information has its lifecycle, which inherently informs its optimal value window. As a result of the critical role information plays in everything, this lifecycle must be intelligently managed to maximize its highest and best uses when the data is most relevant, timely, and actionable for decision-making, problem-solving, and opportunity realization.

To illustrate, the business information lifecycle starts with capturing, storing, sharing and accessing real-time data from business transactions conducted with customers, partners, vendors, investors, and employees in compliance with goals, priorities, and applicable rules and regulations. Sales order data must be captured and stored in the appropriate data store for accounting and finance purposes, analytics modeling, and sales compensation. sales order data must also be designed and stored according to its entity-relationship and data flow diagrams to relate to other business events, such as the sales and marketing campaigns that generated the original sales leads and opportunities. And the inventory management databases are used to fulfill the orders, decrement the inventory master, update the financial journals, and compensate sales representatives.

Finally, to capture and manage the essential customer and product master-reference data needed to enable important data management responsibilities and expectations. Recall that master and reference data are typically identified by naming conventions using keywords like *type, code, list, id*, etc., as either prefixes or suffixes.

Subsequently, sales executives, managers, and analysts must have appropriate access permissions to these data to collaborate with coworkers and better serve customers. Similarly, accounting, financial planning & analysis personnel require access to the related accounting and finance data for budgeting, forecast, and accounting purposes. These business roles rely on IM-IT trade professionals like data architects, developers, business analysts, and database administrators to enable business-critical data capture(Table 6), storage (Table 7), real-time usage, and access capabilities (Table 8).

Table 6 - *Methods of data capture*

Type	Example
Barcode scanners	Self-check at local grocery store chain
Manual data entry	Retail inventory validation audit counts
Electronic data interchange (EDI)	Real estate sales transactions
Optical character recognition (OCR)	Digitalization of medical records folders into medical information systems
Voice recognition	Dragon Naturally Speaking software
Downloads from internet data marketplaces and data brokers	Dun & Bradstreet Corporate Hierarchy Reporting

Table 7. Means of data storage

Type	Example
Onsite/On-Premise (e.g., disk drives, magnetic tape)	The firm decides to keep data onsite for highly sensitive, highly regulated data such as national defense contractors.
Public Cloud	Computing hardware and networking equipment are operated and owned by outside vendor products like Amazon Web Services or Microsoft Azure.
Private Cloud	Hardware and networking equipment is set up in the Client's data center or at a hosting provider.

Table 8. Types of data access

Type	Example
Read-Only	A User can read or view a company's financial statement data.
Read-Write	A User can update or write new data into a database.
Restricted	Only specific personnel can access this highly sensitive data, such as military planning documents.
Private	Very narrow access permission to particular individuals, often associated with product formulations, unique trade secrets, and other proprietary information.

The Information Management Engine

Access to real-time data — defined by quick-to-immediate turnaround between data capture and usage — is worth special attention. Real-time events include things like point-of-sale purchases, social media posts, inventory shipments and receipts, weather radar data, traffic light singles, satellite imagery, data from seismometers for tracking earthquakes, and many different kinds of actual occurrences.

As a result, many computer applications are specially designed to manage real-time use cases. Because real-time use cases are typically at the front lines of an organization's purpose and values, they are usually touch points between an organization and its customers or vendors. Applications like Salesforce and SAP process real-time sales transactions, purchase orders, inventory shipments and receipts, customer service events, billing, invoicing, and accounting transactions.

These real-time production applications must be online and available to process and store critical business transactions and signal-point events at the moment they occur. Think about the sensors in your automobile that capture and send real-time data to your vehicle's computer and transform that data into useful information about speed, engine temperature, fuel level, battery life, outside temperature, or GPS navigation turn-by-turn instruction to inform you of real-time or near real-time conditions both inside and outside of your vehicle. Just like we depend on this information from our vehicles' computers to help us make good decisions and drive safely, business organizations need real-time production information to make accurate, data-driven decisions and inform downstream dependencies required to win customers and compete in target markets.

Assure Business Information Lifecycle Management

Application developers, data, and solution architects work closely with operations support engineers to ensure real-time production applications are always available when needed by front-line managers, supervisors, teams, and individual personnel. This is why real-time application systems owners rarely allow access to activities not directly related to its primary function. For instance, enabling large report queries to process on a real-time order processing application can severely slow down the applications' ability to process their primary business transactions and negatively affect customers.

At this stage of its information lifecycle, real-time data is the essential input source of core business process workflows, so they must be protected from adverse impacts like large analytics queries. Typically, large analysis queries are processed on systems solutions dedicated to this need for trend analysis, predictive modeling, diagnostic discoveries, and preventative investigation.

As a result, real-time data demands strict quality controls, particularly at the initial point of capture and storage. Think about the prospect of your vehicle's fuel level sensor delivering inaccurate information to your dashboard while traveling across a vast desert without fuel stops! This would likely cause immediate concern and a plan to fix it. This analogy is not too far from the seriousness of specific data needed to flow into the value delivery train for critical day-to-day decision-making. For instance, data engineers, architects, scientists, and analysts deliver downstream analysis and support capabilities that transform real-time transactional event data into actionable intelligence and insight for senior leaders and investors.

Data Processing Extract, Transformation and Loads (ETL)

After the initial activities to capture, store, and provide real-time access to the data needed to run the day-to-day operations, the business information lifecycle shifts to the need for downstream dependencies to understand and inform the meaning of the data events into actionable insights. This is where key data management personnel develop and maintain extract, transformation, and load cycles. For instance, point-of-sales data is captured and transmitted in raw form to its real-time application system. It then interfaced with inventory and financial modules to register impacts to product inventory and updates to accounting journals.

Farther down the data lifecycle path, some individual data elements are transformed or calculated into new data elements to track essential metrics like revenue, profit margins, cost-of-goods sold, and customer satisfaction. In some large to medium-sized organizations, data are transformed into hundreds of process performance measures to be managed by the appropriate team or individual. These ETL cycles are established in data processing operations called *job schedules*. These are designed to ensure data flow from and to the right place, process, and person who needs it when needed and, in the format, and definition they need.

Information technology professionals, like database administrators, application developers, and business analysts, work hard to ensure these job schedules are set up, monitored, and measured for optimal effect. They provide "air-traffic control" to prevent schedule collisions and minimize business disruption.

Assure Business Information Lifecycle Management

As a result, some professionals often rotate the responsibility to monitor and alert on job status during 24-hour processing windows of "on-call" duty.

To help minimize the risks, they design data quality checks into these job flows at the point of ingestion or at rest in the target database and within the organization's top reports, dashboards, and scorecards. In addition, some teams buy or build automatic fail-over capabilities and backups when criticality calls for always-on, 24-hour-a-day, and seven-days-a-week uptime. Data at this stage of its lifecycle is critical to its owners and generally at optimal potential value for insight analysis, artificial intelligence, robotic process automation, and machine learning because it is mined for context and meaning to key decision-makers.

The transformation of data into intelligence builds information value capable of monetarization. Information brokers such as credit bureaus gather and sell data about consumers, investors, organizations, and institutions to various marketers, who ingest the data into various modeling engines. Have you ever wondered what happens to your phone number after you purchase a product from the store? Why do they ask for it beyond registering your warranty? What is the purpose of tracking cookies on your internet browsing; how does it help to improve services? Many of these data uses are benign and respectful, disclosing intended benefits and allowing you to opt-out. However, one should always be mindful of the value of this data lifecycle stage to those who possess it.

Backup, Retention, and Retrieval

Business continuity planning, day-to-day

operations, workflow process improvements, and regulatory compliance obligations are demand requirements to back up the organization's most critical data assets and retain them through risk management, data retention policies, and compliance regulations. And this must be enabled with the capability to retrieve and restore the data in a manner usable by the appropriate stakeholder in the event of a major disaster resulting in data loss or breach.

Consider how Hurricane Sandy flooded data centers in New York City in October 2012, impacting significant clients. Or the Microsoft heat spike incident of 2013 caused a major outage of some software applications, like MS Outlook. There are many other disastrous impacts on data networking and storage infrastructure, from weather events to security breaches and other unplanned events.

So, cybersecurity, data governance, and data quality control analysts must collaborate with various risk managers to ensure critical data is routinely backed up and retained according to preset job schedules and random audits. Again, through efficient "air traffic control activities." This collaboration is essential and is often practiced in mock disaster exercises to help guarantee the organization's readiness for potential catastrophic issues. For example, many Data Centers survived the epic flooding from Hurricane Harvey in 2017 due to robust disaster avoidance and recovery planning.

It is also essential to consider that different kinds of data can have unique retention requirements. For instance, some regulations require customer transactions to be retained for five years or more, depending on the country and jurisdiction. This is important because things change in the real world.

New products may have been introduced since the last data restore; the customer master database demographics may have changed. Because people get married, some get divorced, some change their legal residence, some change their names, etc.

Any changes such as these must be considered in the data restoration and recovery strategy. This data is usually stored in some historical database outside the real-time production system. This practice helps to ensure the real-time production system is kept up with enough historical information; this slowness could negatively impact transaction volume, payment processing, and customer experiences.

Therefore, recovering data from archival repositories is as important as backing it up and requires significant due diligence. If substantial changes have occurred in technology infrastructure, such as when data columns are added or deleted from databases between the time data was archived and the time it is needed for recovery. Or the business model could have changed significantly, rendering certain data elements obsolete, meaning that ITM professionals must carefully coordinate the mapping of the old historical data into the new format and structure to retain meaning and context for the transactions or events that the data represents. This is another reason organizations must invest in the talent and growth of core IT-IM trade professionals: to ensure sufficient skill and experience to handle unplanned business scenarios.

Obsolescence and Final Disposition

The lifecycle-of-things dictates an inevitable phase of obsolescence in the valuable existence of objects. Data, like everything else, become obsolete and irrelevant over time due to various factors, such as new product innovation, new market disruptors, changes in regulatory requirements, and changing industry trends. Obsolescence occurs when the object of data is no longer relevant, timely, valid, representative, or otherwise indicative of an active fact above and beyond the satisfaction of all legal and policy requirements.

Data Management trade professionals, like Data Engineers, Architects, and Analysts, help to ensure that data obsolescence is planned and accounted for in the organization's official data strategy for monitoring and managing critical attributes like data Create_Date, Last_Modified_Date, Status (Active or Inactive) and applicable data retention policies to track the useful life of particular data objects.

It's important to remember that obsolescence does not necessarily mean permanent removal or deletion; digital assets can be stored indefinitely, and data storage costs are relatively cheap. Meaning data management leaders work closely with key stakeholders to define the final disposition of certain data assets.

In addition, it is imperative to refrain from comingling obsolete data with active, current data. This can lead to negative impacts on decision-making and problem-solving. This safeguard is one of the responsibilities of data quality control personnel, working with application developers and software engineers. Many teams embed quality control scripts throughout the essential data flow processes to ensure integrity at the point of data usage consumption.

Chapter Summary

Business information lifecycle management begins

with a plan to capture business and financial transaction data with consideration of *storage, usage, retention, archival,* and *obsolescence.* Data engineers, database administrators, and enterprise architects collaborate closely with business analysts, project managers, and data scientists to forecast the volume and scope of input data flowing from business activities into computer applications, databases, data factories, data lakes, and data warehouses.

Information, like everything else, has its lifecycle, which inherently informs its optimal value window. As a result of the critical role information plays in everything, this lifecycle must be intelligently managed to maximize its highest and best uses when the data is most relevant, timely, and actionable for decision-making, problem-solving, and opportunity exploitation.

After the initial activities to capture, store, and provide real-time access to the data needed to run the day-to-day operations, the business information lifecycle shifts to the need for downstream dependencies to understand and inform the meaning of the data events into actionable insights. This is where key data management personnel manage extract, transform, and load cycles. For instance, point-of-sales data is captured and transmitted in raw form to its real-time application system. It then interfaced with inventory and financial modules to register impacts to product inventory and updates to accounting journals.

Business continuity planning, day-to-day operations, workflow process improvements, and regulatory compliance obligations are demand requirements to back up the organization's most critical data assets and retain them through risk management, data retention policies, and compliance regulations. And this must be enabled with the capability to retrieve and restore the data in a manner usable by the appropriate stakeholder in the event of a major disaster resulting in data loss or breach.

The lifecycle-of-things dictates an inevitable phase of obsolescence in the valuable existence of objects. Data, like everything else, become obsolete and irrelevant over time due to various factors, such as new product innovation, new market disruptors, changes in regulatory requirements, and changing industry trends. Obsolescence occurs when the object of data is no longer relevant, timely, valid, representative, or otherwise indicative of an active fact above and beyond the satisfaction of all legal and policy requirements.

Perform Information Requirements Lifecycle Management

The management of information requirements is a critical and intricate process that sustains the health and effectiveness of any organization, particularly in this digital age. The term "Perform Information Requirements Lifecycle Management" refers to a comprehensive approach to managing the flow of data and information in a system from the time it was initially conceived until its eventual retirement. This lifecycle management ensures that all information in an organization is timely, accurate, and useful for decision-making, planning, and other essential functions. The importance of Information Requirements Lifecycle Management is multifaceted. Some key focus areas are highlighted as follows:

Informed Decision Making: All decisions made within an organization rely on the availability and accuracy of information. Effective Information Requirements Lifecycle Management ensures that decision-makers can access the most accurate, up-to-date, and relevant information, resulting in informed, data-driven decisions.

Regulatory Compliance: With an increasing number of laws and regulations about data handling and privacy such as GDPR, HIPAA, etc., organizations must ensure compliance to avoid hefty penalties. Through the effective management of the information lifecycle, organizations can monitor and ensure that their data practices comply with all relevant laws, regulations, and industry standards.

The Information Management Engine

Risk Management: By managing the information lifecycle, organizations can mitigate risks associated with data breaches and loss. This process allows for comprehensive security measures at each phase of the information lifecycle, minimizing the possibility of unauthorized access, alteration, or destruction of information.

Resource Optimization: The lifecycle management of information requirements can help identify redundancies and inefficiencies in data handling, enabling organizations to streamline their operations. This results in cost savings and optimal utilization of resources.

Improved Collaboration and Productivity: Having a structured way of managing information requirements ensures everyone within the organization has access to the right information when they need it. This promotes collaboration between different departments and enhances overall productivity.

Customer Trust: In the era where data breaches are common, managing and protecting the data of customers builds trust and loyalty. Proper Information Requirements Lifecycle Management helps to safeguard sensitive customer information, which in turn improves customer satisfaction and trust.

Knowledge Preservation: A well-managed information lifecycle aids in preserving organizational knowledge. It prevents the loss of valuable data, providing a continuous source of knowledge and insight for the organization.

Strategic Advantage: In the competitive business landscape, information is power. Companies that effectively manage their information lifecycle can gain a competitive edge by quickly leveraging their data for strategic planning, trend analysis, and innovation.

The implementation of robust Information Requirements Lifecycle Management is not merely a necessity but a strategic imperative in the information age. As information becomes increasingly integral to operational success, lifecycle management offers an effective route to harnessing its full potential while managing the inherent risks. By emphasizing this discipline, an organization can significantly enhance its decision-making, productivity, and resilience, setting the stage for sustained success.

The next three sections of this chapter outline the major components of information requirements lifecycle management are informed by the author's professional experiences, training, and certification by IIBA® and PMI®; as well as hundreds of hours of diligent research.

Requirements Observation and Planning

The information requirements lifecycle begins with the observational behaviors and inherent curiosity of business analysts in whatever role or job title they have with respect to requirements management responsibilities. Business analysts must develop a deep and unceasing curiosity for understanding the organization they support, its stakeholders' information needs, how its data impacts customer satisfaction scores, its core workflow processes, and key value drivers of revenue, sales, and margins. Barbara Carkenord, the author of *Seven Steps to*

Mastering Business Analysis, wrote, "One of the most enlightening ways for a BA to learn about a business area is to work in or observe the work as it's being performed." [44]

Senior business analysts know from experience that requirements primarily focus on solving particular problems (preferably at the root cause level), answering essential questions, mitigating, and avoiding risks, enabling performance capabilities, research, and innovation, or exploiting available opportunities. They understand how important it is to get requirements right the first time, avoid the additional cost of rework and deliver solutions verified and validated by requirements stakeholders.

They diligently observe, elicit, analyze, and verify clear, unambiguous problem statements, decision logs, question, and answer logs (i.e., FAQs), user stories, or use cases. Because they know primary stakeholder value emotions drive strategic alignment of an organization's performance capabilities to meet core business needs and functional requirements. This is why effective-efficient information requirements lifecycle management is vital to an organization.

This is an active behavior where business analysts invest time to get to know their critical stakeholders through planned and unplanned interactions, constantly assessing barriers, incidences, and opportunities to contribute. They study the industry and track public financial statements, websites, customer reviews, and social media posts. Then they carry this experience and knowledge into crucial project and program

---

[44] Carkenord, B. A. (2009). Seven steps to mastering business analysis (p. 126). Fort Lauderdale, FL: J. Ross Publishing.

initiatives where they demonstrate their trade skills to elicit, analyze, verify, validate, and trace requirements across the entire information lifecycle.

In addition, business analysts must acquire and improve an actionable understanding of demand-side and supply-side information requirements; only when these two components are balanced can actual needs be addressed most thoroughly. In this capacity, business analysts are liaisons between information consumers and producers, including technology delivery and support roles.

For instance, In digital transformation projects, it is important for a business analyst to possess a strong understanding of various information technology solutions. This enables them to effectively translate the business requirements into functional and technical representations. By doing so, they can communicate accurately with IT solution architects, software engineers, application developers, and data quality analysts.

This highlights the crucial role of business analysis activities and skills within organizations that heavily rely on data. Business analysts serve as critical links in the value delivery process, ensuring that organizations can maximize the potential of their information assets.

As mentioned in our earlier chapter on business analysis, this book distinguishes between requirements (must-haves) and requests (like to have). Accurate, reliable, verified, and validated information requirements serve as the business target's bullseye for major project initiatives and ongoing solution performance to plan. Some information management trade persons refer to, Minimum Viable Product (MVP), to distinguish actual functions and features needed now.

The Information Management Engine

What crucial information does the organization need to possess to effectively win and keep customers, as well as capture a significant market share? Similarly, what knowledge is necessary to attract, nurture, and retain top talent within the organization? It is essential to establish clear differentiations between valid requirements and requests, as these distinctions play a substantial role in guiding budget prioritization decisions made by key stakeholders. Any requirements that hold the highest priority should be identified as must-haves and stored within a repository of knowledge or a master database specifically designed for requirements management.

The requirements knowledgebase serves as a foundation for ongoing analysis and data-driven decision-making. It encompasses the organization's historical needs, current must-haves, and predictable obligations, constraints, opportunities, and capabilities. To develop and maintain this critical knowledge base, the senior business analyst must collaborate closely with data scientists and business intelligence developers, either by acquiring existing solutions or building customized ones to suit the organization's unique requirements.

The requirements master knowledgebase is a valuable tool that empowers senior business analysts to capture and monitor noteworthy observations, trends, or patterns emerging in the industry or internal environment. These insights have the potential to impact solution performance and business workflow processes. The knowledgebase serves as a space for analyzing historical patterns of genuine needs and identifying opportunities to leverage predictive analytics where appropriate. This aids in preparing and planning requirements management activities, processes, and procedures, adhering to industry-leading practices. Just imagine the capabilities of machine learning algorithms and artificial intelligence when applied to your inventory of critical needs.

A comprehensive requirements master knowledgebase can be obtained from a reputable third-party vendor (a simple internet search will reveal numerous options), or it can be developed in-house. Regardless of the approach chosen, certain essential identifiers, attributes, and artifacts should be considered. These can include various figures, tables, and elements that can be organized, defined, or customized in any format that best aligns with the organization's specific needs.

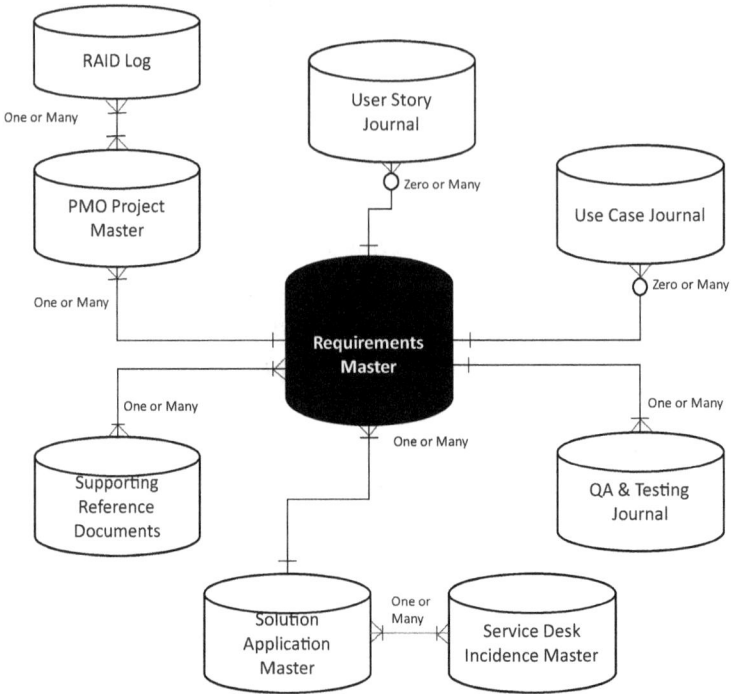

High-Level Requirements Master Conceptual Database Design

RAID Log

One or Many

User Story Journal

Zero or Many

Use Case Journal

PMO Project Master

Zero or Many

One or Many

Requirements Master

One or Many

One or Many

One or Many

Supporting Reference Documents

QA & Testing Journal

Solution Application Master

One or Many

Service Desk Incidence Master

Figure 7 - *Illustration of a requirements master database schema*

Table 9. Requirements Master Fact Table

Column Name	Description
Requirements Master Id (RMID)	Primary-Unique Identifier (PK)
Short description	A short statement of need
Long description	Extended requirement statement
Acceptance criteria(s)	List of quantitative and or qualitative success metrics/checklist items
Type	• Supply-side • Demand-side
Category	• Business Ultimatum • External stakeholder requirement • Internal stakeholder requirement • Solution provider requirement • Functional requirement • Non-functional requirement
Subcategory	• Privacy • Security • Quality • Capacity
Primary purpose	• Answer question(s)

	• Solve problem(s)
	• Enable capability(ies)
	• Exploit opportunity
	• Mitigate/avoid risk(es)
	• Legal compliance
	• Research & innovation
Priority	• Critical
	• High
	• Medium
	• Low
Impact if not completed	• Catastrophic
	• High
	• Medium
	• Low
Urgency	• Immediate
	• High
	• Medium
	• Low
Status	• Completed
	• Rejected
	• In-progress
	• On-Hold

	• Cancelled
Keyword tag(s)	Key word, label, or acronym to group similar requirements
Submitted by	Original person, team, or group expressing the need
Submitted on date	Original submission date into workflow queue, project, or program
Create date	Date of database entry
Created by	The person making the initial database entry
Modified date	The date a modification was made.
Modified by	Person making update
Certification date	Date master requirement was certified as accurate, complete, actionable, timely, relevant, and measurable
Certified by	The person certifying the health of the master requirement
Sign-off date	Date master requirement was signed-off as completed, rejected, or cancelled

The Information Management Engine

Table 10. User-Story Journal

Column Name	Description
Requirements Master Id (RMID)	Primary-Unique Identifier (FK)
User Story Id	Unique Identifier (PK)
As a	Personas, role, or job title
I need	Short need statement
So that	Short statement of intent
Status	• Completed • Rejected • In-progress • On-hold • Cancelled
Project ID	Unique project identifier
Project name	Project title/ label
Submitted by	Original person, team, or group expressing the need
Submitted on date	Original submission date into workflow queue, project, or program
Create date	Date of entry created in the database
Created by	The person making an initial database entry
Modified date	The date the modification was made.
Modified by	The Person making the change
Certification date	The date user story was certified as accurate, complete, actionable, timely, relevant, and measurable.
Certified by	The person certifying the health of the user story.
Sign-off date	Date user story(ies) was/were signed-off as completed, rejected, or cancelled.

Perform Information Requirements Lifecycle Management

The Information Management Engine

Table 11. Use Case Journal

Column Name	Description
Requirements Master Id (RMID)	Primary-Unique Identifier (FK)
Use-Case Id	Unique use-case identifier (PK)
Scenario Number	Unique scenario number per use case (PK).
Scenario Description	A detailed description of the use case scenario
Persona	Persona(s) to whom this use case pertains.
Priority	<ul><li>Critical</li><li>High</li><li>Medium</li></ul>
Impact if not completed	<ul><li>Catastrophic</li><li>High</li><li>Medium</li></ul>
Status	<ul><li>Completed</li><li>Rejected</li><li>In-progress</li><li>On-Hold</li><li>Cancelled</li></ul>
Project ID	Unique project identifier
Project name	Project title/label
Submitted by	Original person, team, or group expressing the need.
Submitted on date	Original submission date into workflow queue, project, or program.
Create date	Date of entry created in the database.
Created by	The person making an initial database entry.
Modified date	The date an update was made.
Modified by	Person making update.
Certification date	Date use-case was certified as accurate, complete,

	actionable, timely, relevant, and measurable.
Certified by	The person certifying the health of the use case.
Sign-off date	Date use-case(es) was/were signed-off as completed, rejected, or cancelled.

Table 12. RAID Log

Column Name	Description
Requirements Master Id (RMID)	Primary-Unique Identifier (FK)
RAID Log Id	RAID Log Identifier (PK)
Short description	A short statement of need.
Long description	Extended requirement statement.
Category	<ul><li>Risk</li><li>Assumption</li><li>Issue</li><li>Decision</li></ul>
Category response type	<ul><li>Mitigation</li><li>Contingency</li><li>Resolution</li><li>Decision</li></ul>
Response statement	Extended statement of responses to RAID line item.
Escalation path	Accountable leadership
Project ID	Unique project identifier
Project name	Short Project Title/Label
Status	<ul><li>Completed</li><li>Rejected</li><li>In-progress</li></ul>

	• On-Hold • Cancelled
Submitted by	Original Person, Team, or Group expressing the Need.
Submitted on date	Original submission date into Workflow queue, Project, or Program.
Create date	Date of entry created in the database.
Created by	The person making the initial database entry.
Modified date	The date update was made.
Modified by	Person making update.
Approval date	Date RAID Log item was approved.
Approved by	The person authorizing RAID Log Item.

Table 13. Test-Case Journal

Column Name	Description
Requirements Master Id (RMID)	Primary-Unique Identifier (FK)
Project Id	Unique Project Identifier (FK)
Project name	Project Title/ Label
Test-case id	Unique Test-case Identifier (PK)
Test-case description	Description of Test
Scenario number	Sequential Scenario Number per Test case
Scenario description	Detail description of the Scenario
Acceptance criteria(s)	Go/No Go Checklist and Thresholds
Test type	• User Acceptance • Unit Test • String Test • System Test

	• Production Warranty
Test lead	Accountable QA Lead
Test team	Responsible QA Team/Test group.
Priority	• Critical • High • Medium • Low
Status	• Approved • Rejected • Parked • Restarted • In-progress • On-Hold • Canceled • Completed
Submitted by	Original person, team, or group expressing the need.
Submitted on date	Original submission date into workflow queue, project, or program.
Create date	Date of entry created in the database.
Created by	The person making an initial database entry.
Modified date	The date update was made.
Modified by	Person making update.
Certification date	The date user story was certified as accurate, complete, actionable, timely, relevant, and measurable.
Certified by	The person certifying the health of the use case.
Sign-off approval date	Date test-case result sign-off was approved.
Sign-off approved by	Person(s) approving sign-off.

The Information Management Engine

Table 14. Supporting Reference Journal

Column Name	Description
Requirements Master Id (RMID)	Primary-Unique Identifier (FK)
Relevant compliance policy	Website/SharePoint URL or Network Drive Location
Project charter	Website/SharePoint URL or Network Drive Location
Business case document	Website/SharePoint URL or Network Drive Location
Functional specifications	Website/SharePoint URL or Network Drive Location
Technical specifications	Website/SharePoint URL or Network Drive Location
Source-to-target data mapping document	Website/SharePoint URL or Network Drive Location
Solution design options	Website/SharePoint URL or Network Drive Location
Solution design decision	Website/SharePoint URL or Network Drive Location
Transition to support agreement checklist	Website/SharePoint URL or Network Drive Location
Support level agreement	Website/SharePoint URL or Network Drive Location
Related workflow process diagram(s) (i.e., swim lane)	Website/SharePoint URL or Network Drive Location
Related data flow diagram(s)	Website/SharePoint URL or Network Drive Location

The Information Management Engine

Table 15. Solution Application Master

Column Name	Description
Requirements Master Id (RMID)	Unique Identifier (FK)
Solution Master Id (SMID)	Unique Identifier (PK)
Short description	A short statement of need
Long description	Extended requirement statement
Type	• Report, dashboard, or scorecard • Cloud-based application • On-premise application • Web portal/website • Software build/buy/upgrade • Hardware build/buy/upgrade • Network build/buy/upgrade • Process improvement • Training and re-enforcement
Priority	• Critical • High • Medium • Low
Impact if not completed	• Catastrophic

	<ul><li>High</li><li>Medium</li><li>Low</li></ul>
Status	<ul><li>In production</li><li>In development</li><li>In QA & testing</li><li>In warranty</li><li>Decommissioned</li></ul>
Service Level Agreement (SLA)	<ul><li>16-hour time-to-respond</li><li>24-hour time-to-resolve</li><li>24–36 hour time-to-resolve</li><li>36–48 time to resolve</li><li>48 hours+ time to resolve</li></ul>
Operating Level Agreement (OLA)	<ul><li>16-hour time-to-respond</li><li>24-hour time-to-resolve</li><li>24–36 hour time-to-resolve</li><li>36–48 time to resolve</li><li>48 hours+ time to resolve</li></ul>
Support contact(s)	Team email, work queue, or individual contact.
Escalation path	Accountable leadership
Solution owner	Accountable person
Process owner	Accountable person

The Information Management Engine

Solution architect(s)	Accountable person(s)
Business analyst(s)	Accountable person(s)
Process engineer(s)	Accountable person(s)
Subject matter expert(s)	Team email, work queue, or individual contact.
Keyword tag(s)	Key word, label, or acronym to group similar requirements.
Create date	Date of the database entry.
Created by	The person making an initial database entry.
Modified date	The date update was made.
Modified by	Person making update.
Certification date	The date requirement solution was certified as accurate, complete, actionable, timely, relevant, and measurable.
Certified by	The person certifying the health of the requirement solution
Sign-off date	Date requirement solution was signed-off as completed, rejected, or cancelled.

Table 16. PMO Project-Program Master

Column Name	Description
Requirements Master Id (RMID)	Unique Identifier (FK)
Project Master Id (PMID)	Unique Identifier (PK)
Short description	A short statement of need
Long description	Extended requirement statement
Priority	• Critical • High • Medium • Low
Impact if not completed	• Catastrophic • High • Medium • Low
Status	• In Progress • On-Hold • Cancelled • In-Warranty • Completed
Project manager	Accountable person(s)
Business analyst(s)	Accountable person(s)

Solution architect(s)	Accountable person(s)
Process engineer	Accountable person(s)
Developer(s)	Accountable person(s)
Subject matter expert(s)	Accountable person(s)
Keyword tag(s)	Key word, label, or acronym to group similar projects, solutions, and requirements.
Create date	Date of the database entry.
Created by	The person making an initial database entry.
Modified date	Date update was made.
Modified by	Person making update.
Sign-off date	Date project was signed-off as completed, rejected, or cancelled.

Table 17. Service-Desk Incidence Master

Column Name	Description
Service Desk Incidence Id (SDID)	Primary-Unique Identifier (PK)
Short description	A short statement of need
Long description	Extended requirement statement.
Category	• On-off Incident • Recurring Incidence • Underlying Problem • Recurring Problem
Urgency	• 48 Hours + • 24-36 • 8-16 • <8 Hours (Immediate)

Severity	Light impact
	Moderate impact
	High impact
	Catastrophic impact
Status	New
	Assigned
	In-progress
	In-escalation
	Resolved
	On-Hold
	Cancelled
	Rejected
Submitted by	Original person, team, or group expressing the need.
Submitted on date	Original submission date into workflow queue, project, or program.
Create date	Date of entry created in the database.
Created by	The person making the initial database entry.
Assigned-to:	Person, team, or group assigned ownership.
Assigned-to date:	Date case assigned to an owner.
Modified date	Date update was made.
Modified by	Person making update.
Date resolved	
Resolution description	A free-form description of corrective action, risk mitigation, or final resolution

The need to deliver the mandates of the business

ultimatum is a vital contribution of the business analysis office and project management office of medium to large-scale firms. Business analysts certified by the International Institute of Business Analysis, or the Project Management Institute have the advantage of a clear roadmap of instruction, guidelines, and professional community support to conduct the mandatory requirements lifecycle management activities to help deliver this mandate.

Specifically, empowering certified, well-trained business analysts and project managers with a well-designed, well-curated requirements master knowledgebase, enables them to contribute significantly to the value delivery train. It helps to supercharge the benefits of their professional development and passions.

The requirements knowledgebase provides a consolidated place of collaboration to capture important notes from observational analysis, focus group sessions, one-to-one interviews, and insights from various meetings they attend. In addition, the knowledgebase enables them to more easily capture and curate learnings from analyzing service desk incidence, data processing events logs, and issue management reports with IT operations support analysts and business relationship managers supporting particular stakeholders, goals, objectives, or priorities.

The requirements master knowledgebase enables them to implement their training with an important tool needed to execute pivotal best practices and tasks — particularly where they benefit from proven requirements management templates, guidelines, and checklists that empower them to master an understanding of the organizations' must-haves so they can easily communicate and collaborate with solution architects and developers. solution architects, software engineers, and application developers help business analyst apply diagnostic and predictive analytics to the requirements master ecosystem to help improve solution designs and performance.

These capabilities are beneficial for medium to large, multi-national corporations. However, it is equally vital for small businesses because they often need more resources to research and understand their business ultimatums in the same way as larger, more sophisticated companies. Nonetheless, business analysts operating in small businesses should build a solid knowledgebase to accumulate, trace and manage the requirements lifecycle in a way that meets their budget constraints. Even a simple Microsoft Access database or Excel worksheet(s) is much better than nothing.

In summary, insightful business analysts understand that having a requirements master knowledgebase enables the organization to gain a more accurate insight into what the business ultimatum is mandating. It helps to reveal actual needs over time and allows the capability to accurately assess solution performance, prepare, plan, and execute requirements collection, facilitation, and quality control.

Requirements Collection-Facilitation, Prioritization, and Quality Controls

The collection, facilitation, and quality control phase of the information requirements management lifecycle is predicated on the capability to elicit, document, trace, and quality control the content of the organizations' most pressing information needs and must-haves. Therefore, presuming the existence of the requirements management knowledgebase, information requirements collections involve these high-level actions:

1. Analyzing existing solution application performance for any known gaps that must be addressed in the current requirements gathering cycle.

2. Analyzing the existing requirements management knowledgebase for relevant insights documented during earlier project initiatives, observations, case studies, and ongoing analysis of available data assets, such as business intelligence reports, the incidence case management database, and data processing event logs. This is an excellent point to spotlight requirements for reusability, traceability, and the everyday needs of relatively static organization functions and processes.

   For instance, most companies maintain an accounting and finance function, human resources, sales & marketing, information technology, and if they produce a physical product, shipping, receiving, and warehouse management. Each of these has certain aspects of its operations that are relatively universal across industries, such as the need for accounting departments to comply with GAAP regulations, the need for sales teams to assign and manage quota-setting plans and geography assignments for sales reps, or the need for warehouse managers to ship and receive products. The basic requirements for these functions are relatively universal and should always be on file in the requirements master knowledgebase for ready access and refinement.

Finally, these universal requirements must always be tagged with a unique identifier, description, and keyword(s) that can be traced from initial capture to solution design and implementation. This allows the requirements to be more easily searched for potential reuse and associated with other pertinent objects, such as named business processes and compliance policies.

3. Reviewing relevant stakeholder needs and preference assessments. This helps determine which requirements-gathering approaches fit best with a given stakeholder's natural communication style, preferences, and level of interest in the initiative.

4. Ensuring a well-established, well-communicated workflow and change management process for entering and updating the requirements master knowledge base. This process should include empowering stakeholders to directly submit initial requirements or enable the transfer of high-priority work requests, issues, incidents, or problem tickets from the case management system via application interfaces (APIs) in preparation for requirements prioritization and demand management.

5. Preplanning requirements gathering and confirmation event logistics, such as time and date for in-person or virtual conference room invites for focus group sessions and or one-to-one interviews, finalizing the attendees or participant list for surveys or questionnaires, assigning session note taker(s), observer(s), timekeepers, and facilitator(s).

6. Assigning specific individual(s) responsible for actively quality-checking requirement

submissions for all critical attributes and
content necessary for prioritization, analysis,
design, traceability, testing, and reusability.

7. Conducting the requirements gathering and
   confirmation events(s).

8. Summarizing all notes, finalizing quality
   checks, and communicating session results to
   crucial stakeholders for confirmation and
   official sign-off.

9. Preparing final requirements package for
   transition to solution lifecycle management
   options analysis and solution design phase.

10. Officially closing the phase with hand-
    off to solution analysis and design, verifying
    that all standard in-phase process checklists
    have been completed and that the initiative
    sponsors have signed off on the successful
    completion of accurate, complete, relevant, and
    timely documentation, collaboration, and
    communication of the organization's mission-
    critical information needs and must-haves.

In support of this high-level list of activities,
all critical stakeholders must be engaged and
actively available to participate when and where
needed during this stage of requirements lifecycle
management. Notably, key stakeholders must be
involved in large-complex digital transformation
projects. I recall a time during a process
transformation project for a large multinational
corporation when a specific team leader disinvited
one of the critical service providers from his
requirements-gathering sessions. The result was that
a significant deliverable still needed to be met. And
what made it worst was that this particular
individual lied about what happened (or at best, came
down with a case of selective amnesia) and disowned

his decision, and causing the company extra time and expenditure to recover that particular deliverable.

I share that egregious example only to make the point that information requirements gathering, and facilitation is as much of an art as it is a science; it requires certified professionals who can regularly balance patience, perseverance, empathy, and core competency to facilitate important initiatives through a range of genuine human emotions, decision consequences, and situational awareness. This is one of the main reasons that I emphasize consistent, ongoing senior leadership support for the core ITM trade practices. Unfortunately, too few business analysts receive the senior leadership support they need to add their maximum value potential to the organization.

This is one reason to advocate for treating business analysis, project management, and solution architecture as vital trade practices requiring training and development in multifaceted aspects and dynamics to deliver value back to stakeholders. When the situation gets complicated, too often some set of detractors resorts to destructive behaviors, so it is essential to have well-trained practitioners who have unwavering support from senior leaders, to anticipate unwelcome dysfunction. They must have the tools to evidence the behaviors' negative impacts on essential value chain deliverables.

The requirements prioritization and quality-controls aspects of this phase help to ensure that only the most critical and best-prepared needs are transitioned to solution lifecycle management. Even though different organizations use the prioritization method that works best for them, they all have these elements in common:

The Information Management Engine

1) An input list of needs and demands from stakeholders. Note: This list should include the needs of solution providers where known.

2) A set of prioritization criteria and a scale of evaluation for their needs.

3) A cutoff line above which submissions are accepted and below which submissions are placed in a backlog for later review or rejected outright.

4) A cutoff time/window beyond which no additional inputs are accepted for a given project or process cycle.

5) A quality-control readiness checklist to ensure submissions contain all the essential elements and attributes needed to ensure they are accurate, complete, timely, relevant, actionable, traceable, and, if required, reusable.

6) One or more accountable individuals with final sign-off decision authority.

Transition to Solution Lifecycle Management

The transition phase of requirements lifecycle management begins with the planned execution of ongoing requirements maintenance for relevancy and, eventually, obsolescence. Senior business analysts ensure that requirements deployed in active solution applications are reviewed periodically and assessed for continuous fit-for-purpose to the consuming organization.

Again, the requirements knowledge base is essential to this capability. The status flag is set accordingly in the requirements knowledge base if and when requirements are deemed obsolete. This process stage is a significant factor in the lifecycle of things.

Transition to solution lifecycle management is a collaboration between business technology users and information technology providers, that is, between demand-side needs and supply-side requirements to fulfill the need, facilitated by seasoned business analysts. Business analysts are critical liaisons between business process owners, data owners, organizational change managers, IT solution architects, software engineers, quality assurance analysts, application developers, and service desk support agents.

In addition, some organizations deploy business relationship managers (BRM) to serve this liaison role between business technology consumers and information technology providers. Some business analysts perform the role of business relationship managers because of their skills, talents, and experience. Organizations that train, support, and deploy IT business analysts, business relationship managers, and demand-side business analysts typically have a robust, effective transition plan to solution lifecycle management.

The primary purpose of these relationships during the transition from requirements lifecycle management to solution lifecycle management is to ensure that no prioritized requirements fall between the cracks and to confirm that requirements analysis and solution design options are effectively correlated to the organization's value delivery goals and objectives. An accurate readiness checklist, proven process templates, and techniques guided by these experienced business analysis teams with a deep understanding of the organization, its core processes, and its information technology capabilities will significantly enable a successful transition.

Chapter Summary

To summarize, the information requirements lifecycle begins with observational behaviors and inherent curiosity of business analysts; in whatever role or job title they're in with requirements management responsibilities. Business analysts must develop a deep and unceasing understanding of the organization they support, its stakeholders' information needs, how its data impacts customer satisfaction scores, its core workflow processes, and key value drivers of revenue, sales, and margins.

The collection, facilitation, and quality control phase of the information requirements management lifecycle is predicated on the capability to elicit, document, trace, and quality control the content of the organizations' most pressing information needs and must-haves.

The transition phase of requirements lifecycle management begins with the planned execution of ongoing requirements maintenance for relevancy and, eventually, obsolescence. Senior business analysts ensure that requirements deployed in active solution applications are reviewed periodically and assessed for continuous fit-for-purpose to the consuming organization.

Perform Information Solution Lifecycle Management

The information management solution lifecycle is the total of all activities to ingest prioritized, certified (verified and validated) information requirements and dependencies into optimized control processes. These solution management control processes involve developing and analyzing design options, selecting the preferred option, constructing or purchasing, testing/validation, training, implementation, organization change management, and continuous improvement through ongoing performance evaluation, governance, and, ultimately, obsolescence.

The core purposes of an information solution's lifecycle management include ensuring that it delivers consistent, reliable answers to essential questions; enables insight into persistent problems; empowers effective research & development; converts time-sensitive opportunities into beneficial outcomes; and provides value to primary stakeholders. ITM professionals strive to manage the solution's lifecycle in a manner and method agreeable to the solution's end-users, in addition to the solution providers and ongoing support teams. That is to continuously balance supply-side and demand-side requirements with the capability to perform effective, efficient solution lifecycle management.

At its core, managing the lifecycle of information management solutions is essential for organizations because it enables the resolution of problems, provides answers to questions, and facilitates the transformation of information into actionable outcomes. By controlling, coordinating, collaborating, communicating, and governing these solutions, organizations can derive numerous benefits. These benefits extend beyond the initial objectives and include higher net promoter scores, increased sales volume, improved conversion rates for marketing campaigns, enhanced efficiency in inventory management, greater employee satisfaction, and various other key performance metrics.

To fully leverage these benefits, I strongly recommend capturing three important ratios in the requirements management knowledge base. This will enable the application of artificial intelligence, machine learning, and potentially robotic process automation while adhering to appropriate standards and procedures. Doing so will enhance the organization's ability to make data-driven decisions, optimize processes, and maximize the value obtained from the information management solutions implemented.

This challenge excites dedicated ITM trade-persons because it motivates them to deliver sustainable products and services. They're excited to create, configure, or improve solutions that provide value to others and give them a strong sense of accomplishment. It's similar to an artist creating a fantastic painting and applying her unique signature in the lower corner of the artwork. For those who enjoy ITM, it's motivational to help deliver something that remains in active status for years. Individuals who manage the roles of core ITM tradecrafts do well to remember this in their hiring and development practices.

For this reason, It is crucial to view information solution lifecycle management as a comprehensive ecosystem that encompasses various interrelated components. These components include processes, people (with their skills, experience, and motivation), and the IT infrastructure, which consists of hardware, software, telephony, networks and communications, data, and governance. By considering this holistic approach to solution lifecycle management, organizations can address the requirements and dependencies that arise at different stages of the information flow, distribution, and utilization. This ensures a cohesive and well-managed system that maximizes the value and effectiveness of the information solutions implemented.

Information requirements are not isolated entities; they are interconnected and shared across various teams, functions, or departments within an organization. These requirements form a network of interconnections, akin to chain links. For example, the information needs identified by a sales team can have implications for other departments such as finance, marketing, and product development. These departments need to take into account the sales team's requirements when making pricing decisions, creating financial forecasts, assessing shipping capacities, and managing inventory.

By recognizing the interdependence of information needs, organizations can ensure effective collaboration and coordination among different teams and departments. This interconnectedness helps facilitate efficient decision-making processes and enables a holistic approach to addressing information requirements throughout the organization.

Therefore, the transition from information requirements lifecycle management to solution lifecycle management involves cross-functional project teams of business analysts, solution architects, user-experience designers, quality assurance analysts, and business subject-matter experts conducting detailed reviews of the in-scope requirements captured in the requirements management knowledge base. These reviews entail a set of iterative collaborations to confirm transitional understanding, validate expected outcomes, features, and functionalities, and identify potential risk and mitigation options as a condition of the transition to solution lifecycle hand-off.

Solution Options Analysis and Preference Selection

Upon successful transition sign-off, the solution management elements of the information management organization, especially solution architects, are tasked with detailed analysis of the in-scope requirements, use case scenarios, and or user stories to develop realistic design options and to analyze those options for best-fit under a given set of constraints. Solution Architects familiarize themselves with the contents of the requirements knowledge database for existing solutions to ensure continuity, cost savings, and minimize potential rework.

Solution architects, developers, and data scientists use techniques like fishbone diagrams for root-cause analysis; they employ modeling techniques like Monte Carlo simulations, develop proofs-of-concept or prototypes, and brainstorm for options idea generation. **Table 18** shows a high-level assessment of the advantages and disadvantages of five options labeled **A** through **E**. This helps the team evaluate which options have the most benefits with the fewest disadvantages; in this case, option B is the clear winner.

Table 18. Design Options Analysis

Design Goals and Objective Statement		
Decision Option	Advantages	Disadvantages
Option A	• Advantage1 • Advantage2 • Advantage3	• Disadvantage1 • Disadvantage2 • Disadvantage3 • Disadvantage4
Option B	• Advantage1 • Advantage2 • Advantage3 • Advantage4 • Advantage5 • Advantage6	• Disadvantage1 • Disadvantage2
Option C	• Advantage1 • Advantage2 • Advantage3	• Disadvantage1 • Disadvantage2 • Disadvantage3
Option D	• Advantage1 • Advantage2 • Advantage3	• Disadvantage1 • Disadvantage2 • Disadvantage3
Option E	• Advantage1 • Advantage2 • Advantage3 • Advantage4	• Disadvantage1 • Disadvantage2 • Disadvantage3

Once viable options have been identified and assessed for their pros and cons or advantages and disadvantages, an assessment is made to determine the preferred option using a predefined set of decision criteria. **Table 19** illustrates this example, where options A through E are evaluated against a backdrop of ten decision criteria the project team defined to determine which option best delivers the expected outcomes for primary stakeholders and solution end-users.

These criteria should answer questions like: Do we have the budget to complete this option? Is building the solution internally or purchasing a third-party product more advantageous? Do we have the requisite talent, time, and tools to execute and maintain the solution over time? Is this option reversible in the case of unintended negative consequences?

The decision on a preferred design option is significant and should be thoroughly vetted; it will

179

commit valuable time and resources that may not be easily substituted or recuperated. Therefore, projects with substantial investments must conduct careful due diligence in this preferred option selection. The construction industry adage "measure twice, cut once" definitely applies. Agile project teams must be diligent and skillful at doing this because they must balance speed and agility with forethought and planning. It's about "doing it right the first time or doing it fast at the risk of doing it over."

Table 19. Preferred Option Selection Criteria

Design Goals and Objective Statement					
Decision Criterion	Option A	Option B	Option C	Option D	Option E
Criteria #1	✓	✓	✓	✓	✓
Criteria # 2		✓			
Criteria # 3		✓	✓		✓
Criteria # 4	✓	✓		✓	
Criteria # 5		✓	✓	✓	✓
Criteria # 6	✓	✓	✓		✓
Criteria # 7	✓			✓	
Criteria # 8		✓	✓	✓	✓
Criteria # 9	✓	✓	✓		✓
Criteria # 10	✓		✓		✓

Solution Application Development, Purchase or Configuration

After the project team has selected the preferred design option and secured the requisite sign-off from all vested stakeholders, they are prepared to execute their decision to build or build. The Solution construction option for any part of the IT infrastructure will involve relevant experts in that technology area. For instance, if the preferred solution option requires a communications network upgrade, network engineers are preeminent for this phase. Similarly, application developers and architects become preeminent if the preferred solution design calls for a new software application. Regarding a business process architecture solution requirement, business process engineers, business architects, and subject matter experts are also essential to solution construction.

During this stage of the solution lifecycle, project managers and solution architects rely on a valuable tool called RASCI analysis. This tool plays a vital role as it helps them coordinate and control the specific individuals who are accountable and responsible for the most crucial tasks. These tasks are essential for meeting the project's completion objectives and ensuring the success of the solution's performance, as outlined in the project charter, project plan, and work-breakdown structure.

The RASCI tool, presented in **Table 20**, proves instrumental in reducing confusion within the internal project team. By clearly defining roles and responsibilities, it minimizes misunderstandings between technology delivery teams and stakeholders. This enhances communication and collaboration, leading to a more efficient and effective execution of the project, ultimately increasing the likelihood of achieving desired outcomes.

I strongly recommend that program management offices own and facilitate the RASCI artifact for high-profile, large medium-to-large investment solution initiatives. These RASCI documents should include all significant phases of the project lifecycle, including critical transition hand-offs and ongoing support upon completion of the official project end date. Business analysts, project administrators, and process SMEs are particularly helpful in maintaining RASCI documents because the document must be kept up to date to reflect changes in the project team and role changes in the organization.

Table 20. Solution Design & Implementation RASCI Chart

RASCI Chart

Tasks	Information Requirements Solution Design & Implementation								
	Project Manager	Project Administrator	Business Analyst	Solution Architect	Software Developer	UX Developer	QA Analyst	Subject Matter Expert	Sponsor
Milestone A									
Task 1	C	C	R	C	C	C	C	C	A
Task 2	C	R	R	A	C	R	C	C	I
Task 3	A	R	C	C	R	C	CI	C	I
Milestone B									
Task 4	R	R	C	I	R	C	A	C	I
Task 5	R	R	A	I	R	R	R	C	I
Task 6	C	C	A	C	R	R	RC	C	I
Milestone C									
Task 7	C	A	I	C	C	R	R	C	CI
Task 8	A	C	C	C	C	C	C	R	R

Responsible – Accountable – Sponsor/Support - Consulted - Informed

Tracking each component of the solution development in a buy scenario means tracing each core component of the purchase to its underlying requirements documented in the requirements management knowledge database. This helps to ensure referential integrity and traceability at this critical juncture for later reference in the solution performance evaluation stage. There must always be a plumbline that stretches from specific questions, problems, and needs to preferred design to construction or purchase and ultimately into quality assurance testing and validation.

This traceability and lineage are intended to ensure the preferred design option are verifiably implemented to facilitate answers to thoughtful questions, helping intelligent the resolution to targeted issues and problems, or enabling business teams to convert opportunities into actual benefits and stakeholder value. Experienced Solution architects, business analysts, and process managers know that subsequent solution performance evaluation for value delivery and continuous improvement is predicated on how well solution development and delivery teams performed during this crucial time.

These ITM professionals accrue and refine working checklists of success criteria, templates, techniques, policies, and standards, increasing their chances of achieving the expected solution performance. Depending on budgets and other resource constraints, several vendors offer products and services to assist them. ITM teams conduct comparative analyses of vendors' products and services using tools like request-for-proposals, and request-for-quotes, which help to narrow down offers to the one that best fits solution performance requirements and quality standards.

Information Quality Assurance and Regulatory Compliance

Information quality assurance and regulatory compliance functions are important throughout the information management lifecycle, but they hold particular significance during solution testing and validation. Information requirements can present themselves in various scenarios, each with its own independent variables to consider. Therefore, it is crucial for information quality assurance to accurately test the most likely and high-impact scenarios to ensure compliance with real-world conditions that the solution aims to address.

To achieve this, quality assurance analysts work closely with business analysts, data security analysts, process engineers, and subject-matter experts. Together, they define and document test case scenarios early in the requirements management lifecycle to verify and validate that the solution performs as expected. Scenario-based test scripts are developed, which can be processed by automated testing and validation engines. Effective collaboration among these roles is carefully monitored and facilitated by program, project, and people managers.

During the testing and validation cycles of project initiatives, project managers assign test leads to oversee the essential activities and tasks necessary to obtain stakeholder sign-off. This is where the RASCI Chart can be utilized to drive the critical path to success. Stakeholder sign-off is important as it confirms that all test case scenarios have been executed and successfully passed or that appropriate contingency plans and steps have been taken to address test cases that do not meet acceptance criteria.

Regular project status communication is vital to keep stakeholders informed about test case results and disposition decisions that impact them. Information solution testing and validation involve iterative cycles of Plan-Do-Check-Act (PDCA) until a final disposition is reached. This is especially crucial for data quality testing.

Since data quality serves as the foundation for all aspects of information value delivery, it is crucial to rigorously validate its accuracy, completeness, conformity to applicable standards, timeliness, relevancy, and absence of unnecessary duplication. Project teams must prioritize implementing sustainable data quality controls throughout the solution lifecycle, particularly for Personally Identifiable Information (PII) and Protected Health Information (PHI). PII refers to combinations of attributes that can identify an individual, such as name and Social Security number, home address, personal email address, bank account number, or phone number. PHI encompasses health-related data that can be used to personally identify someone, including personal medical records, health transactions, or billing records containing PII.

Many organizations have dedicated teams of experts in data quality management who collaborate with information governance and data security professionals. Together, they ensure that the solution adheres to critical regulations, standards, and policies relevant to its scope and purpose. Some of these regulatory compliance mandates include:

- **General Data Protection Regulation** of 2018 (**GDPR**). A wide-ranging European Union data privacy and security framework designed to ensure that the private, personal data of their citizens are well protected from undue and limited to responsible, accountable, traceable use on an as-needed basis by any company or organization, regardless of the organization's location. For example, GDPR regulates whether data about its citizen can be stored on computer hardware or devices outside of particular EU countries.
- **California Consumer Privacy Act** of 2003 (**CCPA**). Similar to GDPR in that it is designed to protect its residents' private data from being

used in a manner the consumer has not explicitly authorized and levies heavy fines on organizations operating in California that violate those rights. For example, CCPA mandates that California residents maintain a right to have their data removed or erased, the "right to be forgotten."

- **Health Insurance Portability and Accountability Act** of 1996 (**HIPAA**). A set of rules including federal privacy safeguards to set national standards for patient electronic health record privacy and security protections. The U.S. Department of Health & Human Services regulates HIPAA. The scope of these regulations encompasses data sourced from healthcare transactions, patient visits, medical records, or any other mechanism or process that captures, stores, or shares the personal health information of any U.S. citizen. More information on HIPAA can be found at HHS.gov/hipaa/index.html.

Increasingly, regulations across different countries involve significant risks to business owners, investors, senior managers, and other primary information management stakeholders, such as the Personal Information Protection and Electronic Documents Act of 2000 (PIPEDA) in Canada, or the Act on Protection of Personal Information in Japan (APPI), and the General Data Protection Law of 2018 (LGPD) in Brazil.

ITM professionals must incorporate regulatory requirements testing, validations, and training into their information solution quality and security management projects and programs. Violations of these laws can lead to heavy penalties. For example, anyone proven to have perpetrated a willful violation of

Perform Information Solution Lifecycle Management

HIPAA can face a criminal penalty of up to $50,000 and up to one year in jail! Proven violations of GDPR can cost an organization four percent of annual revenue or a fine of up to $22 million!

Solution Application Training and Move-To-Production

After successful validation of solution quality and security, ITM professionals must closely collaborate with the organization's training teams. In medium to large companies, they also work closely with the change management organization to ensure successful deployment and adoption of necessary process, procedure, or work instruction changes. Thorough planning and coordination throughout the solution performance lifecycle greatly benefit project and program teams in this regard.

Training for upgrades to existing solutions or the addition of new functions and features will focus on introducing and establishing literacy and adoption of the new capabilities within the current operating environment. However, when the information solution is new to the organization, training objectives and success measures are more comprehensive. They include the functions and features required to deliver the capabilities identified in the requirements management knowledge base. This training may also encompass any process or policy changes mandated by the new solution design.

Moreover, information solution training can extend beyond initial project releases and should be managed in plan-do-check-act cycles. Some solutions are complex enough to warrant a regular and comprehensive training and evaluation curriculum. This ensures the achievement of the necessary information solution proficiency and literacy levels.

The Information Management Engine

For example, a new manufacturing shop floor process quality control solution with artificial intelligence and robotic process automation features might require introductory training, intermediate-level training, and advanced training for those demonstrating higher proficiency. This training helps expand the use of high-end functions and features of the solution to significantly reduce the defect rate in the manufacturing process and improve product quality.

Successful training and organizational change management programs are planned, executed, and reviewed using qualitative and quantitative metrics. The insights gained from these reviews are fed back into solution improvement feedback loops. The objective is to prioritize, monitor, measure, and manage information literacy, education, and development intentionally. A highly effective training rollout significantly enhances the likelihood of delivering information value to stakeholders after the Move-To-Production (MTP) implementation stage of the solution lifecycle.

The transition to the Deployment or MTP phase of the project represents a critical control point for solution owners and managers. Their sign-off indicates that all significant critical-path activities and solution readiness criteria have been met or appropriately addressed. It confirms that solution sponsors and owners have certified the successful design, build or procurement, testing, and validation of prioritized requirements. It also verifies the completion or ongoing progress of relevant training, necessary documentation, and proper change management.

As this stage of the information solution lifecycle is where stakeholders expect ongoing benefits and perceived value, solution adoption and support play a

188

significant role in solution performance management, monitoring, and evaluation. Particularly when solution performance managers shift their focus from the initial pre-project business case to post-project evidence of expected benefits and value realization.

Insightful senior executives, such as chief financial officers, chief information officers, and chief data officers, understand the urgency and importance of following through on the promises made in the business case. They routinely hold the program management office leadership team accountable for delivering on the commitments outlined in the original or adjusted business case. This habit of pre-, in-, and post-project benefit analysis is crucial for organizations of any size to exercise and develop. Information solution projects can be costly in various ways, and demonstrating and presenting the value of information solution delivery can be challenging. However, with deliberate practice and iteration, value analysis and effective communication become more regular and natural. It becomes the usual way of doing business.

Business case commitments often span multiple years and depend on the information solution's performance and service management excellence over that time. Unfortunately, project teams often deliver a specific set of features and functions to an organization only to quickly shift their attention to the next project. This can lead to a lack of focus and follow-through on existing commitments to ensure value is generated, measured, and maintained.

As a result, senior business analysts, program managers, and process owners inherently understand that the move-to-production implementation represents a critical milestone for the management, service, and support operations of information solutions.

The Information Management Engine

Solution Service Management and Support Operations

Once an information solution is actively in use, the operational excellence of its service and support becomes crucial in realizing the expected value. An information solution that is frequently unavailable during critical times cannot deliver any value. Likewise, an information solution with a helpdesk that responds slowly to urgent end-user needs offers little benefit. Value cannot arise from an information solution if its support engineers are insufficiently trained to address pressing user questions and resolve high-impact issues promptly. The net present value of an information solution is contingent upon the service operations team equipped with the proper tools and technologies to deliver excellent support.

Successful information solution service management requires a healthy synergy of professionals with strong interpersonal skills, core competencies in relevant technologies, effective training programs, and ongoing leadership support. Without proper management and resources, information service, support, and control operations can be challenging and frustrating for everyone involved, including service providers and stakeholders. In fact, the unfavorable conditions have led many operations and support experts to resign out of frustration and disappointment. Hence, it is crucial to highlight some critical elements of information solution service and support management.

First and foremost, it is essential for leaders in information solution management to closely monitor the emotional well-being of their teams and individual personnel. This responsibility is particularly important for managers overseeing teams engaged in internal or external customer interactions. Managers must address any issues that negatively affect morale, professional development, or commitment to excellence. They should know their employees well enough to identify early signs of burnout and demonstrate care and concern for their teams' well-being, just as they prioritize business results. Sometimes, this means helping support engineers, agents, analysts, and administrators effectively handle challenging situations or difficult individuals.

Secondly, information service and support teams greatly benefit from the effective use of business intelligence reports, visualization dashboards, and scorecards. These teams typically have access to valuable data from processing logs, helpdesk tickets, and survey results, enabling them to identify patterns and perform root cause analyses. The emphasis should always be on quickly identifying the underlying causes of recurring incidents and taking preventive measures. Whether the root cause is human error, lack of training, technology issues, or a lack of accountability, problems must be resolved at their source.

Additionally, business intelligence capabilities offer service and support operations teams a deeper understanding of the organization's workflow processes that they help deliver and sustain. They can learn about how sales teams source critical data and how it is integrated and aggregated for sales cycle planning. They can also identify patterns in helpdesk ticket logs that empower them to suggest new business requirements and consult stakeholders in preparation for future solution releases.

Business intelligence reporting enables service and support teams to visualize and comprehend the dependencies between business metrics and internal service operations performance metrics. For example, financial planners cannot generate timely quarter-end forecast reports if the information solution experiences significant downtime during that reporting cycle. Similarly, time-sensitive sales and marketing campaigns may be hindered if the information solution's level-2 support has long response and resolution times.

In essence, business performance metrics rely on the metrics of information solution service and support operations. Having a foundational understanding of both sets of metrics allows service and support teams to grasp their contributions to the organization and comprehend the significance of the information solution's performance outcomes. Over the years, I have observed that IM service and support personnel who actively seek to understand these dependencies, share their insights with colleagues, and take ownership of their role in delivering value, enjoy credibility and career success. They become sought-after subject-matter experts and internal consultants for important project initiatives. Many of them exemplify the concept of blue-collar technology workers.

Lastly, the information solutions' service management portfolio should include a specific set of core services, as depicted in **Table 21**.

Table 21. IT Service & Operations Portfolio

Service and Operations Portfolio	Encompasses all activities and tasks necessary to
Service event management	• Schedule, coordinate and manage data processing events, including source-to-target extracts, transformations, and load procedures.

	• Plan, coordinate, and perform operating system upgrades, patches, testing and validation, scheduled audits, and move-to-product releases. • Coordinate communication and recovery of unplanned outages or other unscheduled events.
Incidence and problem management	• Communicate, coordinate, resolve, and prevent unplanned outage or service disruption incidence and any underlying problems in the solution infrastructure that inhibit the organization's productivity, operational efficiency, and capabilities-to-perform primary stakeholder value delivery.
Access permissions management	• Coordinate, control, grant, revoke, or suspend secure access to the organization's information solution assets. • Document, distribute, train, enforce, and maintain information solution access policy compliance.
Applications support management	• Ensure all software applications perform by established service-level agreements (SLAs) and support measurable information solution value delivery.
Disaster recovery management	• Contingency planning, coordination, practice, execution, communication, and recovery from catastrophic, unplanned solution disruption, including natural disasters, malicious data security

	intrusions, or unintentional major disruption mistakes.
IT infrastructure operations management	• Perform routine console monitoring, • Perform automated health checks and standard operating procedures for equipment startup, shutdown, • Perform data storage and restoration procedures, data archival and deletion, • Install upgrades and patches for hardware devices, specifically computers, phones, laptops, tablets, and communications network equipment.
Communications management	• Communicate service-level performance results, plan and coordinate scheduled downtime, and monitor and notify affected stakeholders of issues and risks discovered in Automated Alerts and Log file analysis. • Proactively inform senior leadership of potential risks to solution performance continuity, stability, and reliability. • Proactively monitor and notify accountable senior leadership of all severe incidence of non-compliance to regulatory obligations detected during the ordinary course of solution support operations.

Perform Information Solution Lifecycle Management

Solution Adoption and Change Management

Information management solution adoption often depends on the effectiveness of organizational change management. Implementing changes in information technologies, workflow instructions, standard operating procedures, or established processes can be complex for organizations of any size. ITM practitioners who understand this demonstrate empathy, understanding, patience, and mutual respect for teams or individuals struggling with the change.

For instance, the installation and deployment of technologies like artificial intelligence, machine learning, advanced analytics, and robotic process automation can be perceived as a threat to job positions, leading to mistrust and concern among those performing roles within the scope of these technologies. This is not limited to traditional blue-collar jobs; these technologies are increasingly capable of automating white-collar repetitive tasks such as customer service phone calls, invoice generation, and accounting journal entries. Employees are aware that labor costs are typically among the highest expenses for any organization. Given this backdrop, information solution providers must be perceptive and diligent in preparing the organization for change and planning how it will impact individuals and their families.

In the case of digital transformation solutions, it is best to assign this foresight and preparation to dedicated experts with diverse experiences in managing organizational change. Many organizations choose to outsource this function to external systems integrators who have a team of professionals specializing in organizational change management.

Information solution changes are inherently challenging because they aim to address unanswered questions, resolve deep-seated problems, and exploit opportunities promptly. Without addressing these issues, an organization, especially in highly disrupted and competitive industries with slim margins, is unlikely to survive for long.

Consider the scenario of an information solution that has been in use for many years, with individuals who have extensive knowledge of its operations. Some may believe that the solution works fine and does not require significant changes. However, accountable business leaders and senior managers recognize the need to keep pace with rapidly advancing technologies and competitive market pressures. They understand that the solution lifecycle may have reached its limit and a change is necessary.

I emphasized earlier that the working relationship between human resource representatives, team leaders, and people managers is crucial in organizational change management triggered by information solution innovations. Digital transformation initiatives, by nature, represent change and require thorough planning, consistent communication, transparency, and trust.

When mishandled, the organization can experience significant attrition of valuable talent and skills, leading to diminished benefits from the change. Therefore, insightful information managers strive to design solutions that align with the strengths of both the technologies and the workforce. When such a balance is not feasible, leaders, coaches, and change agents within the organization must play an active and constructive role in helping essential personnel prepare for and embrace the change. This may involve offering new opportunities to displaced employees and providing retraining for new job roles. It is essential to handle these transitions with sensitivity and care, not only for the affected employees but also for their families and loved ones.

The objective of organizational change management and solution adoption is to achieve strategic alignment between the interests of employees and the needs of investors and business owners. By earning returns on invested capital that exceed the cost of capital, these stakeholders contribute to the organization's survival and growth.

Solution Application Governance and Performance Management

At this stage of its lifecycle, the information solution application is not only in evidence, but it is mapped and traceable to the requirements it's designed to deliver, the questions it's designed to answer, and the problems it's designed to resolve via the requirements and solution management knowledge databases. These knowledge databases trace prioritized, certified requirements, user stories, and use case scenarios to the organization's value drivers of its goals, objectives, and key performance indicators.

By definition, applying an accurate solution to a business problem or an answer to an urgent question is fundamental to survival and growth. These applied solutions' governance necessitates developing and adopting a practical, efficient set of standards, rules, policies, and procedures to facilitate performance excellence. Without this governance, many organizations cannot achieve or sustain best practices like specific ISO standards; because they have little or no natural mechanism to guide them objectively through inevitable changes, challenges, risks, and bottlenecks of day-to-day operations and processes.

Imagine your favorite sport, played without rules of fair play and ethical conduct or without experienced referees in place to steward the game through the highest standards of its competitive challenges. That would surely take much of the fun out of it, especially if you're on the losing team!

Indeed, the rules of the game matter, and the practices and principles deployed in the game can determine whether your team wins or loses. In competitive sports, compliance with rules, guidelines, policies, and procedures, officiated by dedicated, ethical, well-trained personnel to support the game's players, coaches, and staff, makes up the core of the guardrails to help ensure the game itself survives and grows.

Similarly, solution application governance is the set of all activities, tasks, principles, and practices necessary to ensure information management teams, technologies, and the workflow processes they enable are harmonized, coordinated and managed to deliver the highest standards of performance excellence, quality assurance, and value delivery. This set of governance attributes and properties can be summarized into three hierarchical domains. Each of the three requires leadership due diligence, priority, and attention; the flow of accurate, complete, relevant, timely information is the lifeblood of any organization and a competitive advantage to those that manage it best.

Our model's three major information solution application governance domains are *foundation, transformation, and excellence.* Figure 9 illustrates a model of information management solution governance that highlights the hierarchical relationship of foundation services' essential enablers of the capability to transform data into information, intelligence, and insightful action. In turn, these transformations power the delivery of high-performance methods, metrics, and means into realized actual value as a consequence of actual enablement execution and transformative causal actions. The entire model is predicated on the principle of an applied governance capability to "watchdog" and ensure that every element of the information solution ecosystem is harmoniously calibrated to produce the experiences customers and employees desire most and exceed returns investors and owners expect.

The Information Management Engine

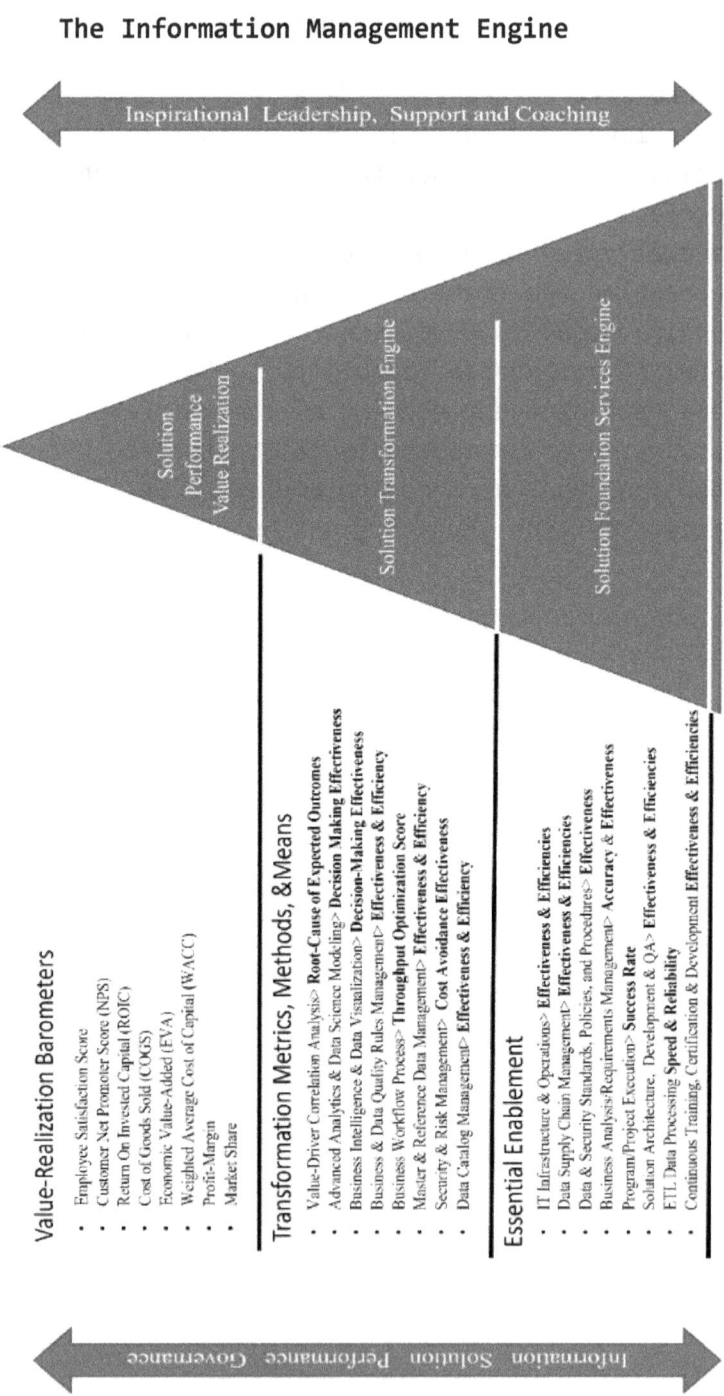

Figure 8 - *IM Solution Governance Hierarchy*

Perform Information Solution Lifecycle Management

The *foundation* domain is the set of personnel, technologies, activities, tasks, processes, policies, and procedures required for effective-efficient monitoring, alerts, recovery, and preventative actions to ensure the underlying solution infrastructure is sound and reliable and that it is consistently delivering high-quality data into the transformation domain. The foundation domain is essential enablement. It is so fundamental and indispensable to sustainable stakeholder value delivery that one can easily compare it to the necessity of electric power and flowing water to our homes, places of work, worship, and other habitable building.

Think about the most straightforward act of walking into a room and flipping the light switch for the lights to turn on. Most people would not give that a second thought compared to the reason they entered the kitchen in the first place. And that's not even considering all the utility workers, equipment, vehicles, and facilities required to deliver electric power to their kitchens.

However, the second the lights do not turn on, for whatever reason, most people's priority will turn to the need to fix the lights. The problem may be as simple as a blown light bulb or fuse. Or it could be something more serious like a blown power station or, worst, a cybersecurity hack. In either case, the infrastructure behind electricity services is foundational to all higher uses of it. Thankfully, a cadre of trained personnel, processes, monitoring, and recovery technologies are in place to dispatch a fix that keeps the lights on.

Similarly, information technology network and database administrators routinely monitor interface console screens for real-time computer hardware, network, or database performance alerts. These consoles can be compared to a dashboard in a car or the control panel an airplane pilot uses to fly a plane. To illustrate, many companies invest in automated systems monitoring, email, and phone alerts and coordinate 24-by-7 work shifts to ensure no critical performance threshold is breached that would negatively impact the organization's day-to-day functions.

Seasoned IT administrators are trained and skilled at understanding which alerts to action immediately versus those that require more in-depth attention from higher levels of support and analysis expertise. Individuals who manage this personnel need a certain degree of emotional energy and intelligence to help ensure top talent is developed and retained to accelerate and maintain the time-to-respond and time-to-resolve predefined thresholds within service-level agreements and proactively inform stakeholders of potentially damaging impacts. The solution performance elements of the organization's requirements management knowledge database are excellent for cross-referencing foundation domain learnings into service improvements.

The foundation domain comprises core critical service capabilities, including IT infrastructure and operations, data supply chain management, data, and security standards, policies, and procedure governance. And business analysis and requirements management, program and project execution, information solution architecture, development, quality assurance, and ETL data processing efficiencies. A successful program of continuous training, professional certification, and developing the organization's information quality culture makes these services productively sustainable.

Perform Information Solution Lifecycle Management

Solution governance at this level is equally critical and should be managed harmoniously with essential information management elements of the foundation domain. At this point, I think it's necessary to distinguish between effective-efficient governance and successful information management. It's the difference between sports players and officiating personnel. The governance (officiating) personnel's primary role is to ensure the organization's investments in foundation information management resources, methods, and means provide a solid, reliable platform to convert inputs into desired outputs and transform stakeholder expectations into value realization. It's probably not a good idea to put the fox in charge of guarding the hen house.

Transformation is the second primary domain of information solution application performance governance. This domain encompasses the personnel, technologies, activities, tasks, processes, and procedures required to transform data into information, intelligence, and deeper insights. Insights are designed to improve objectives like financial forecast accuracy, decision-making effectiveness, advanced sentiment analysis of customer preferences, and improved correlation analysis for the root causes of desired effects.

The transformation domain also encompasses innovations in program, project, and process management improvements, such as master data and reference data management, cost avoidance through effective cybersecurity and risk management. This domain ensures that the organization's workflow process business rules are well-throughout, tracked, and enforced to complement and harmonize with relevant data quality rules compliance.

The Information Management Engine

Like the foundation domain, the transformation domain encompasses essential monitoring of predefined performance thresholds and information quality control limits. For this reason, the transformation domain features a set of analytical dashboards, scorecards, and models specifically designed to improve decision-making accuracy, answer essential questions, solve long-term and short-term problems, and exploit available opportunities promptly.

In addition, transformation domain governance ensures that critical decision-makers, strategists, and thought leaders have the best intelligence regarding the latest industry trends, emerging regulations, and other external factors beyond their control. Senior business analysts, seasoned program managers, and business and solution architects intuitively understand their roles in maintaining awareness of external factors. They know how imperative it is to perform as the organization's lighthouses to warn and mitigate potentially adverse effects and facilitate positive exploitation of opportunities some external factors may present.

The governance team's primary role in the solution application transformation domain is to facilitate adherence to high-performance standards, policies, and best practices like those found in well-known standards organizations. They are the lighthouse night watchmen, tower guards, and hall monitors for unwarranted or unintended deviation from the root causes of primary stakeholder perceived value realization.

Value realization is the third primary domain of information solution application performance governance. This is essentially the "prove it" stage of the information solution lifecycle. Our solution performance governance model highlights a few measures a commercial organization seeks to evidence the benefits of its investments in information solution applications. These are a few of the intended consequences of selected objectives, goals, and an organization's unique value propositions.

Primary stakeholders such as customers, investors, and employees demand a perceptible degree of satisfaction and fulfillment in exchange for things they value, notably their time, effort, and financial resources. So, the value realization domain of our information solution governance hierarchy encompasses two core elements of proof:

1. **Body of evidence:** *"I believe it when I see it!"* Credible statistical metrics and measures provide objective evidence of particular causes and effects when calculated and calibrated from high-quality data, proven concepts, and research experiments from the application of targeted science. Analytics are vital in this regard because it helps to evidence answers to questions and solve problems. If, for instance, the question remains unanswered and the specific issues unresolved, stakeholders rightfully are skeptical of the net outcomes these metrics and measures purport to indicate. Stakeholders want visual proof that they receive a fair return for things they value.

   Defining the input variables that impact solution performance is critical to evidencing value realization, including the quality of the inputs. Such as the availability of talent, skills, and experience when and where needed to make a difference. Or the quality and reliability of the information management technology chosen during the request-for-proposal stage of a buy-v-build solution design evaluation.

Additional credence can be assigned to the thoroughness of business analysis and requirements definition, the effectiveness of the project management execution, and the effectiveness of the end-user training as leading indicators of eventual solution application adoption and performance. Similarly, the degree to which workflow processes comply with crucial business rules and data processing pipelines adhere to data quality rules also provides insight into the solution's capability to produce desired outcomes.

Therefore, ITM practitioners must remain committed to sharing the input parameters and governance controls necessary to validate that the information solution application verifiably contributes to stakeholder value realization metrics and measures. The evidence of these deliverables should be traceable to things like Earnings Statements, Sales Dashboards, Net Income Statements, Cash Flow Statements, Employee Satisfaction Scores, Productivity gains, Operational efficiency gains, the actual reduction of Product Quality Defects, and increases in Customer Net Promoter Scores.

2. **Experiences that Matter**: *"I believe it when I feel it!"* – I believe there is no substitute for a particular type of customer, investor, or employee experience. Particularly those positive experiences that can be measured with one or more of the five senses and associated with feelings of joy, happiness, fulfillment, excitement, laughter, or gain. Business organizations and even Non-Profit companies must constantly survey and validate whether their products and services consistently deliver these experiences to their primary stakeholders. These

are experiences that matter! What inspires Customer Loyalty, Employee Retention, and Investor commitments?

Organizations that depend on high-performance information technology solutions to deliver these targeted experiences warrant information management professionals that embrace their unique roles in this challenge. They must help ensure that front-line, essential workers and their managers have the best foundation data services and data transformation engines available for decision-making support, process optimization, product innovation, and professional training programs to perform to high standards of excellence consistently.

Solution Application Decline and Obsolescence

The lifecycle-of-things over time mandates that an information management solution application will eventually enter the decline stage and require planned obsolescence. Once the solution no longer adds value according to its intended design, investment goals, and expected outcomes, it becomes unfit for its purpose.

Determining the exact date of this stage is challenging because various factors can trigger it. These include new product innovations disrupting the industry, increased competition leading to reduced profit margins, emerging government regulations, or a sudden scarcity of essential resources.

These factors emphasize the need for a comprehensive approach to information management ecosystems. Enterprise architects, IT strategists, and portfolio managers have the specific responsibility to study, anticipate, and effectively plan for the decline and obsolescence of information solutions. Their aim is to minimize unintended consequences and ensure business continuity. They monitor and manage product releases, upgrades, and patches until they observe diminishing returns on investments in terms of resources and time. These activities encompass planned updates to metadata catalogs, requirements, and the knowledge databases of solutions management.

If a new solution replaces the old one, a transition project must be initiated and executed according to established high-quality performance standards and continuous improvement cycles applied to the old solution. Continuous improvement serves as the driving force that motivates dedicated information management professionals to strive for excellence and deliver tangible value to primary stakeholders.

Chapter Summary

After receiving sign-off for a successful transition, the information management organization's solution management elements, particularly solution architects, are responsible for conducting a detailed analysis of the requirements, use case scenarios, and user stories within the defined scope. Their objective is to develop realistic design options and evaluate them based on given constraints. Solution architects familiarize themselves with the contents of the requirements knowledge database for existing solutions to ensure continuity, cost savings, and minimize the need for rework.

Once the project team selects the preferred design option and obtains the necessary sign-off from stakeholders, they are ready to execute their

decision to either build or buy the solution. If the
decision is to build, specific technological
expertise must be available to complete the
construction. For example, if the preferred solution
option requires a communications network upgrade,
network engineers play a crucial role during this
phase. Similarly, application developers and
architects take the lead when a new software
application is part of the preferred solution design.
In cases involving business process architecture
requirements, the involvement of business process
engineers, business architects, and subject matter
experts is essential for solution construction.

Throughout the information management lifecycle,
information quality assurance and regulatory
compliance functions are critical. However, their
significance is particularly pronounced during
solution testing and validation. Information
requirements often manifest in various scenarios with
independent variables to consider. As a result,
information quality assurance must thoroughly test
the most likely and high-impact scenarios to ensure
compliance with real-world conditions that the
solution intends to address.

Once the solution undergoes successful quality and
security validation, ITM professionals collaborate
closely with the organization's training teams. In
medium to large companies, they also work closely
with the change management organization to ensure
successful deployment and adoption of required
process, procedure, or work instruction changes. This
emphasizes the importance of thorough planning and
coordination throughout the solution performance
lifecycle.

When an information solution is officially in
active use, its service and support operational

excellence becomes crucial in realizing the expected value. An information solution that is consistently unavailable during critical times adds no value. Similarly, a solution with a helpdesk function that cannot respond promptly to urgent end-user needs does not provide significant benefits. The expertise and training of first and second-level support engineers are crucial in swiftly addressing pressing end-user questions and resolving high-impact issues. The net present value can only be achieved when support operations teams have the right tools and technologies to deliver excellent service.

The adoption of information management solutions often relies on the effectiveness of organizational change management. Changing information technologies, workflow instructions, standard operating procedures, or established processes can be complex for organizations of any size. Insightful ITM practitioners understand this and demonstrate empathy, understanding, patience, and mutual respect for teams or individuals who may struggle with the changes.

According to the natural law known as the lifecycle-of-things, information management solutions will eventually enter the decline stage and require planned obsolescence. When a solution no longer adds value according to its design intent, investment objectives, and expected outcomes, it is no longer fit for its purpose or useful life. This highlights the necessity for organizations to anticipate and plan for this stage, ensuring the continuous delivery of value throughout the solution's lifecycle.

PART IV: Encourage Information Technology Careers

In the fascinating realm of Information Management, an range of cutting-edge technologies awaits young minds ready to shape the future. From the intricate designs of Artificial Intelligence (AI) to the precision of Robotic Process Automation (RPA), the ever-evolving landscape offers an unparalleled canvas for those seeking a career at the forefront of innovation. Imagine harnessing the power of Machine Learning to predict trends, unravel complex patterns, and make data-driven decisions that transform industries. This dynamic field encompasses Data Science and Advanced Analytics, where raw data metamorphoses into strategic insights that drive business success.

At the heart of this excitement lies Artificial Intelligence, a field that ignites the imagination and challenges the boundaries of what's possible. As AI systems learn, adapt, and evolve, young professionals have the chance to delve into the creation of intelligent algorithms that mimic human cognition. Imagine crafting AI-driven chatbots, optimizing recommendation systems, and even contributing to self-driving cars that reshape transportation. The possibilities are endless, and the thirst for creative problem-solvers in this field is unquenchable.

Robotic Process Automation is another game-changing aspect of Information Management. This technology involves automating repetitive tasks through intelligent software robots, freeing up human talent to focus on strategic thinking and value-added activities. The young minds who step into this arena can revolutionize industries by streamlining operations, increasing efficiency, and unleashing unprecedented productivity gains.

Machine Learning, a subset of AI, brings data to life by enabling systems to learn and improve from experience. This technology is at the core of recommendation engines, fraud detection algorithms, and even healthcare diagnostics. Embracing a career in Machine Learning means contributing to innovations that have the potential to revolutionize every facet of modern life, from personalized marketing to life-saving medical breakthroughs.

Data Science and Advanced Analytics are the bedrock upon which all these technologies rest. Young individuals with a penchant for data-driven exploration can unearth valuable insights from vast datasets, revealing trends and opportunities that shape business strategies and decisions. The power of data is immense, and the professionals who wield it skillfully have the ability to drive transformation on a grand scale.

The realm of Information Management beckons young minds to dive into a world of limitless possibilities. The latest advances in Artificial Intelligence, Robotic Process Automation, Machine Learning, Data Science, and Advanced Analytics promise not only exciting careers but also the chance to be at the forefront of technological revolutions. Whether you're passionate about creating intelligent algorithms, automating processes, unraveling data's secrets, or making breakthroughs with AI, this field offers a canvas where innovation and imagination know no bounds. So, if you're ready to shape the future, an Information Management career is your gateway to a world of endless innovation and impact.

IT Management — A Strategic Career Choice

Managing information technology, teams, programs, processes, and professionals is interesting, challenging, rewarding, and very much in demand. The U.S. Bureau of Labor Statistics employment projections for 2021 through 2031 highlight "Computer and information systems managers" among its top occupations with the most job growth at a median annual wage of $159,010.

According to the U.S. Bureau of Labor Statistics (n.d.), information technology managers "plan, direct, or coordinate activities in such fields as electronic data processing, information systems, systems analysis, and computer programming." [45] Similarly, data science managers, software application development directors, vice presidents of data governance and cybersecurity, and chief information officers (CIOs) are compelling career aspirations for those wanting to contribute, grow and develop in an exciting and critical career.

Information technology management is a strategic choice for those who understand the primal nature of information and the absolute base level need that all organisms and organizations have as a prerequisite for survival and growth. IT management is also a strategic choice for those pursuing excellence who want to make a difference in moments that matter.

---

[45] U.S. Bureau of Labor Statistics. (n.d.). Computer and information systems managers. Retrieved March 6, 2023, from https://www.bls.gov/ooh/management/computer-and-information-systems-managers.htm

IT Management — A Strategic Career Choice

Information technology, particularly microprocessors, appears in some essential use cases.

The information technology management discipline is broad and deep, containing career options across virtually every major industry, institution, and society in the world. If a technology product includes a microchip, it's information technology related. And most modern human-made products were directly or indirectly designed, developed, and delivered using information microprocessing chips. This illustrates an enormous opportunity for those with the desire, willingness, and dedication to pursue a career in information management.

Think about the effort and energy required to land a human being on the surface of Mars and the information processing power needed to accomplish that. Think about healthcare and medical situations, where computer processing capabilities can determine a patient's life or death in partnership with human training, skills, and experience. This is particularly true during moments that matter, like major medical surgery. Or consider the use of precision-guided military equipment or submarines operating at depth in the deep oceans. Each of these fields requires information processing technology; consequently, they all require skilled, dedicated, emotionally intelligent managers of that technology.

The fact that information technology is constantly changing, amid the sheer volume of data, creates a compelling career opportunity for those who embrace change and the challenge of continuous improvement. As a result, information technology managers must develop foundational core competencies in one or more areas of computer technology, process, development, architecture, or engineering disciplines.

Because IT managers must have the tools and skills

needed to lead the activities of teams of individual contributors, these core competencies can include a working knowledge of programming languages like SQL, JAVA, C, R, Python, and many others. Some IT managers may possess a core competency in hardware operations, networks and communications technologies, software engineering, data science, cybersecurity or solution architecture, data quality or metadata management, and technical writing.

Computer and information systems managers must become conversant in the language of the technologies, processes, and professions within the scope of their span of control and influence. They need this foundation to serve their teams best, help individual contributors resolve technical and process issues, and sometimes navigate difficult situations. This is particularly true for those managing fast-paced teams on the front lines of helpdesk operations, customer service, or sales support.

Computer and information managers must fully understand and embrace the Business Ultimatum and the data quality culture and help to create the value-delivery mindset within the team. They should strive for a working knowledge of the organization's financial statements, goals, objectives, value drivers, and key performance indicators.

This means information technology managers must develop the skills, experience, and emotional intelligence to engage directly with other business managers accountable for specific business performance metrics and value drivers, like sales managers, product quality supervisors, directors of product marketing, or chief financial officers. Such managers and teams outside the information technology disciplines understand and embrace their dependencies on accurate, reliable, timely data. They may seek to develop and supply it themselves if unsatisfied with IT service and support. This is typically called *shadow IT* and, if not managed correctly, can create tremendous risks, extra costs, and dysfunction between teams. However, if managed correctly, shadow IT can be an excellent source of innovation and a valuable extension of the IT department's capacity.

Information technology managers ensure delivery of high-quality intelligence in the form of valuable answers, solutions, and opportunities. They also coach, develop, encourage, advocate for, and sponsor talent in their organization, helping them to grow and develop into seasoned professionals and prepare them for moments that matter.

The manager's role is to reward, recognize and encourage continuous improvement and learning. It is a compelling opportunity for individuals with the aptitude, attitude, and desire to lead, coach, train, and develop others across various organizations and industries. At the time of this writing, information technology managers have career opportunities in industry sectors like education, healthcare and pharmaceuticals, human resources and payroll processing, politics and government, product manufacturing, retail and fashion, finance, insurance and accounting, supply chain, transportation and logistics, entertainment and sports, and information technology.

ITM Careers in Education

I am hard-pressed to think of a more honorable and vital occupation than educator. It makes modern civilization possible. Education is the opportunity to inform, encourage, support, and develop young minds to thrive and grow into their unique potential to fulfill their life's dreams. I greatly respect those who chose early childhood education because these educators give children a solid foundation for success.

Educational institutions at all levels depend on access to computerized technology and information systems that help prepare students for life in the digital age and beyond. The opportunities for information systems managers include directors of computer departments, who coach, lead and develop programmer analysts, database and network administrators, computer lab administrators, software quality assurance analysts, and testers.

Educational organizations also need information security managers to lead, coach, and develop data security engineers, compliance analysts, and internal auditors. Cybersecurity is vital in higher education because many institutions partner with government agencies on vital research and development initiatives in aerospace, defense, pharmaceutical, and other susceptible areas. Colleges and universities collect significant amounts of personal information about students and staff in database systems that can be hacked or subject to ransomware attacks.

All educational institutions and facilities need experienced information managers to train, develop, teach, and oversee course curriculums. This can be rewarding in many ways for those who have a passion for teaching and love working with information technologies. It's a beautiful way to give something back for the care and support one may have received on their career journey.

Many job boards and search services are available to those whose interests lean toward the education and training industries. Social media platforms provide additional exposure to interest groups, blogs, and podcasts. (For instance, ZipRecruiter published a list of the cities with the highest pay for educational technology positions). [46]

In January 2023, more than 10,000 IT-related management opportunities were available in education, including:

- Supervisor, Business Program Management and Support

- Director of Enterprise Project Management Office

- Associate CIO, Project, and Technology Consulting Services

- Division IT Manager

- Senior IT Manager, Enterprise Applications Development

- IT Senior Director/CISO

- Manager of IT Applications and Development

- IT Epic Director/UKHC

- Manager, DevOps Engineering

- IT Sr. Manager

- Information Technology Manager

- IT Manager - Web Design and Development

---

[46] ZipRecruiter. (2023, January 15). Top ten highest paying cities for educational technology jobs. Retrieved March 6, 2023, from https://www.ziprecruiter.com/blog/10-highest-paying-cities-for-educational-technology-jobs/

- Transportation IT Systems Director

- End-User Computing Manager

- Manager IT Service Management

- IT Director for the Eloy Elementary School District

ITM Careers in Healthcare and Pharmaceuticals

Healthcare IT is vital to progress in medicine, disease, and stress control. This industry collects vast volumes of data of staggering complexity with major privacy and security considerations. Healthcare is heavily regulated and constantly undertakes massive research and development initiatives.

A search on LinkedIn job boards reveals thousands of healthcare-related IT jobs, like solution architects, application managers, senior healthcare business analysts, IT program and project managers, information governance managers, IT directors, and many more. Managing these roles to ensure high-performance excellence can significantly affect the hiring organization, employees, customers, and patients. Therefore, managers in this space must be well trained and usually need some healthcare-related experience in their background and training.

Fortunately, many resources are available for those wishing to build or supplement their exposure to healthcare IT opportunities. These include college and university degree programs with internships as well as professional certification programs such as the American Medical Informatics Association's Certified Health Informatics Professional designation.

According to several recruitment sites, a

healthcare IT professional's average salary ranges between $80,000 and $126,000 across the United States in 2022. As in most careers, this salary range increases with education and on-the-job experience.

ITM Careers in Human Resources and Payroll Processing

Human resources and payroll are among the most consequential IT management areas outside the information technology function because HR and payroll are jointly accountable for successfully administrating employee salary, benefits, training, engagement, and retention.

HR and payroll departments depend on information technology management to ensure they can process and administer their duties. They coordinate closely with IT to ensure that payroll is consistent and reliable 100% of the time. There are few more significant blows to employee morale than missing payroll or issues with critical health benefits. The data processing and business intelligence requirements for HR and payroll must be diligently managed throughout its lifecycle. This requires strict adherence to high performance standards for information management professionals and their solution applications.

Many medium- to large-sized firms leverage cloud-based, third-party payroll software applications like Workday or ADP to support employee administration needs. HR and IT managers coordinate and control these engagements through contractual agreements and vendor management. In addition, HR and IT managers must ensure that critical employee data flows downstream to all necessary business intelligence functions that provide resource forecast analysis and decisions support. These information flows must be constantly monitored for consistent data integrity and timeliness to support employee engagement, talent acquisition and retention, reward and recognition awards, and ultimately employee satisfaction and fulfillment.

HR IT manager roles include HRIS directors, IT business analysis managers, HR IT project managers, and HR solution application development managers. In 2022, the average salary for HR technology managers in the U.S. was $170,000, ranging from $136,000 to $204,000 a year.[47] More than 3,000 HR IT-related jobs were listed on LinkedIn in January 2023, all working within a team of professionals led by skilled and experienced information technology managers. Many other job boards, websites, and staffing agencies list considerable IT management postings in HR, benefits, and payroll.

ITM Careers in Politics and Government

The uses of data and information technologies in politics and government are challenging to count. These services range from vetting research on potential government appointees to opposition research between political revivals. The consequence of getting this vetting wrong can be enormously negative. In contrast, the benefit of getting this information right can expose unwanted risks early enough in the process to avoid costly mistakes and therefore requires the very best in computer and information management.

Local, state, and federal government agencies in the United States and worldwide depend heavily on information technology managers to lead the acquisition of new computing and network security

---

[47] Comparably. (2022). HR technology manager salary. Retrieved March 6, 2023, from https://www.comparably.com/salaries/salaries-for-hr-technology-manager

capabilities. They use information systems for almost every aspect of government administration, ranging from screening potential new hires to heavy computational data processing at the National Aeronautics and Space Administration.

Imagine the excitement and challenge of managing the teams of IT professionals responsible for maintaining the computer and networking software and equipment required to send and receive dataflows into and out of the International Space Station. or those managing the IT support teams at large Department of Defense contractors like Northrop Grumman, Raytheon, Boeing, Lockheed Martin, or General Dynamics.

From the Department of Defense and Veteran Affairs to the Department of Health and Human Services and the Federal Emergency Management Agency, government agencies are heavy users of computerized information management technologies such as supercomputers, laptop, smartphones, and tablets. These departments need a cadre of information technology teams and their managers to ensure they can deliver sustainable value-added services to the public and countries they serve.

Computer and information managers working in politics and government must remain on top of regulatory compliance requirements because noncompliance has serious consequences, including global incidents, defamation lawsuits, tremendous privacy and security violation fines, and even incarceration.

According to Indeed.com, the average annual salary for an IT specialist in the U.S. government was $52,000, with a high of $122,000. One would expect an even greater average and range for those managing teams of government IT specialists, engineers, architects, and developers.

The Information Management Engine

ITM Careers in Product Manufacturing

Manufacturing — particularly advanced manufacturing, uses computerized information systems for robotics, artificial intelligence, machine learning, natural language processors, and several use-case applications for microprocessors and signal point controllers. As a result, this industry typically involves a broad range of computer hardware and operating systems.

At one end of this range are small to mid-sized servers for office applications like business intelligence reporting systems, finance and accounting systems, human resource information systems, etc. These can be on the organizations' premises, or the organization can subscribe to cloud-based services.

Medium- to large-scale systems and dedicated controllers are required for certain manufacturing processes. Consider the importance of continuous flow processes to consumer goods and pharmaceutical companies like Procter and Gamble, Pfizer, Moderna, PepsiCo, or Glaxo SmithKline. These organizations' information processing and maintenance requirements are intense — sensor data and signal point data generate real-time analytics essential to sustaining reliable, continuous flow operations monitored by product analysts and technicians.

Finally, there are the supercomputers that companies like Raytheon, Northrop Grumman, and Boeing require to process big-data applications. Information processing technologies and networks are vital to meeting quality specifications, whether using a small computer tablet used by a research lab technician or a giant supercomputer used by theoretical physics.

Information technology managers in manufacturing are accountable and responsible for the results of their team's output and for ensuring their portfolio of information technology infrastructure and workflow processes deliver high-performance standards. They must collaborate effectively with other disciplines, like mechanical and electrical engineers, logistics planners, shop floor managers, product quality managers, and workflow process engineers. The IT manager leads teams of computer engineers, user-experience developers, data quality engineers, and data scientists as the core of cross-functional working relationships under their span of control and influence.

As a result, computer information system managers should learn how to facilitate different teams' efforts, including those that do not report directly to them. Facilitation is vital to efficient continuous process flows and an organization's ability to produce defect-free products. This point highlights the interdependencies between the information systems department, product manufacturing front-line teams, quality control teams, warehouse and inventory control teams, sales and marketing teams, finance and accounting teams, and product design teams.

Information technology managers in manufacturing also help logistics planners create computerized simulation models of the manufacturing, warehousing, shipping, receiving, and inventory management processes. These simulations help business managers understand key parameters and variables affecting the end-to-end process flow value chain. This capability provides an opportunity to conduct "what-if" scenario analysis to improve decision-making and identify optimal process configuration options.

Information technology managers help to facilitate manufacturing process improvement methodologies like Lean Six Sigma, Total Quality Management, Business Process Management, and Plan, Do, Check, Act. These methodologies benefit directly from information processing and management capabilities, providing a competitive advantage to meet the organization's Business Ultimatum.

The product manufacturing industry can be highly competitive, particularly in sectors like consumer goods. Some companies operate within thin profit margins due to factors like supply chain costs, research and development, legal and regulatory requirements, and high labor costs. And product manufacturing environments are highly interdependent and interactive, necessitating process optimization projects and programs that ensure critical resources are applied directly to the value chain within the information ecosystem.

This ecosystem of information, people, and technologies offers an exciting opportunity for individuals to lead and manage. For instance, information technology management in product manufacturing environments requires strong facilitation skills. These facilitation skills are needed to collaborate with challenging colleagues in difficult situations and scenarios. For instance, specific product line machine controllers must consistently and reliably feed data to the analytics engines for effective decision support. Data like this which is highly shared between upstream and downstream teams, departments, and functions, must be documented and mapped in the data catalog for shared understanding and standardized use.

ITM Careers in Retail and Fashion

Retail and fashion IT careers support an ecosystem of processes and technologies including point-of-sale information systems, inventory management systems, invoice and purchasing management systems, computer-aided design, simulation modeling systems, sales management systems, and customer resource management systems. These technologies are essential to researching, testing, purchasing, and selling commodities like textiles, fabrics, and dyes. The industry depends on information technologies to research and develop pricing strategies, forecast seasonal employment needs, plan sales and marketing campaigns, predict television, internet, and radio advertising revenue, and drive inventory turns.

Retail IT teams include application developers, software engineers, IT business analysts, IT architects, and IT project and program managers. In addition, organizations that follow Agile and other hybrid project management methodologies may standardize the roles of Scrum Master and IT Product Owner. In either case, IT team managers and leads are accountable for ensuring their teams are cohesive, highly productive units to support dynamic, fast-paced retail environments, use cases, and user stories.

Duties of IT managers in retail businesses may include:

- Overseeing the training and development of core technical and process competencies required to successfully manage information systems in the retail industry.

- Aligning short- and long-term IT team priorities with business goals, objectives, value drivers, and key performance indicators.

The Information Management Engine

- Proactively managing stakeholder communications and notification for ongoing operational updates, project, and incidence status.

- Managing IT vendor relationships to ensure service level agreement performance is reliably consistent with acceptance criteria.

- Researching and recommending new and emerging technologies to help ensure stakeholder information requirements are consistently delivered on time and within quality specifications.

- Coordinating, controlling, and allocating IT budget across their span of control.

- Ensuring that their teams stay abreast of industry innovations and news that may affect them.

In January 2023, more than six hundred positions were available in retail IT management, including:

- IT Manager - Retailer Applications

- IT Audit Managers

- Manager, IT Vendor Management

- IT Manager - Projects

- Senior Manager - IT Audit

- Manager, Windows System Administrator, and IT Collaboration

- Manager IT Development

- IT Product Manager

IT Management — A Strategic Career Choice

- Vice President of IT (Heavy retail is a must-have)

- IT Manager I (Mobility)

- Manager, IT Help Desk - Hybrid

- It Senior Manager

- IT Manager of Network Security Engineering

- Business-To-Business (B2B) IT Manager

- Senior Manager Product, IT-Retail Technologies

- Technical Support Manager, SaaS Customer Support

- IT Manager - Release and Test Management

- Manager, Application Support - REMOTE

- Senior Product Manager, Supply Chain and Business Systems

- Manager, IT Business Solutions

Such jobs are posted across a wide range of retail stores, operation and logistics departments, and functions. The common thread is a prevailing need for individuals with the interest, aptitude, skills, and experience to fulfill this vital need in the retail industry to help companies reliably deliver the products people want and need to store shelves.

ITM Careers in Finance, Insurance and Accounting Services

Information technology managers operating in finance and accounting industries, departments, and functions are crucial to an organization's ability to comply with local, state, and federal laws and regulations — especially those that protect consumers from unfair trade practices. These regulations include the Equal Credit Opportunity Act, the Home Mortgage Disclosure, the Fair Debt Collection Practices Act, Truth in Lending, and the Privacy of Consumer Financial Information. Federal regulatory agencies in this space include the Consumer Financial Protection Board (CFPB), Federal Deposit Insurance Corporation (FDIC), Financial Industry Regulatory Authority (FINRA), Securities and Exchange Commission (SEC), and the Federal Reserve Board (FRB). Similar regulations and agencies are in place in other developed countries.

These regulatory institutions also require dedicated IT managers, directors, vice presidents, and CIOs to coordinate, control, and collaborate across interdependent organizations to help deliver the organization's mandates and operating charters.

For instance, financial planning and analysis managers in these agencies lead monthly financial forecasts, the annual budget process, and ongoing planning. They prepare monthly financial reporting and analyses for critical decision-makers. Finance IT managers are crucial to a finance or accounting manager's ability to design, code, and process the complex financial models required to analyze the organization's conditions and prepare official financial statements.

Finance, insurance, and accounting companies, departments, functions, and teams depend on effective information technology management systems mainly to comply with applicable laws, policies, practices, and principles guiding their work. For instance, the Financial Accounting Standards Board issues the set of Generally Accepted Accounting Principles (GAAP) that public companies in the U.S. must follow. Fortunately, many software application products are developed in-house to support regulatory compliance.

In many organizations, the sheer volume of daily business transactions and the complexity of some models necessitate robust capabilities to process large data streams and to help the organization respond rapidly to spikes in demand and fraud detection or other increased security risks.

IT managers play a crucial role in planning, executing, and maintaining these capabilities. Based on their experience and working knowledge, they provide internal consulting to ensure compliance and achieve value-delivery commitments, objectives, and goals.

In January 2023, more than 500 IT management jobs were available in finance and accounting, including:

- Senior Manager, Financial Systems

- IT Audit Manager

- IT Manager

- Financial Systems Manager (Remote)

- Senior Manager II, Controllership Technology Accountant

- IT Application Manager

- Workday Technology Manager

- Business Manager, Engineering, and Information Technologies

- Manager, Technology Services Manager

The Information Management Engine

- Manager Finance Systems

- Senior Director Enterprise Financial Information Systems

- Senior Manager of Information Security

- IT Systems Manager

- Enterprise Cloud Risk Manager

- SEC - Information Security Manager

- Manager, TTP Tech Support

- Director, D365 Finance and Operations Technical Architect

- Senior Manager, Business Intelligence and Analytics

- Manager, SAP Financial System Validations

- IT Financial Improvement and Audit Remediation (FIAR) Manager

In 2023, an IT finance manager's average income is $105,230, with a total estimated at $131,014.[48] As with any average, there is headroom in this scale for higher earning potential depending on experience, education, training, and desire.

ITM Careers in Supply Chain, Transportation and Logistics

Supply chain, transportation, and logistics

---

[48] Glassdoor. (2023, January). IT finance manager salary. Retrieved March 6, 2023, from https://www.glassdoor.com/Salaries/it-finance-manager-salary-SRCH_KO0,18.htm

management are core-critical to every aspect of modern society, from getting the kids to school to shipping and receiving vital replacement parts for the Space Station. IT managers are crucial to driving the information requirements and solution application lifecycles to fulfill an organization's needs to schedule, dispatch, and route their chosen modes of transportation by rail, truck, plane, or ship.

Information technology in this sector can be as life-and-death as in healthcare, and it can require extensive computing power to manage the metrics, formulas, and calculations involved. For instance, many agribusiness companies need to calculate the freight weights at the beginning, middle, and end of the journey of particular ingredients that may shift, settle, or evaporate and determine whether it's safe to cross a specific bridge or mountain slope. An airplane shipment planner must know how to formulate the best configuration and stacking pattern to maximize the airplane's stability during takeoff and landing. And think about the skills, experience, and dedication it takes to manage the information ecosystem in air traffic control!

Supply chain management companies depend heavily on advanced technologies, simulations, and sophisticated algorithms to help reduce risks, lower costs, and maximize efficiency. Information technologies can even be found in agriculture, where satellite images help in estimating rainfall levels and crop yields. Farmers and ranchers use this information to modernize and optimize their decision-making about which crops to plant and where or which livestock are best suited for the land on their ranch.

Most medium to large transportation management companies install tracking devices on their trucks, rail car, and ships to enable tracking, security controls, and route analytics. These data represent inputs to data science and simulation modeling tools that are imperative to improving decision-making regarding routes. These decisions can have significant impact on the risk of a particular shipment. Consider, for instance, the dangers to trucks and drivers (or planes and pilots) while distributing products to remote parts of Alaska, or the challenges of delivering important cargo through countries with high crime rates or kidnapping risks.

Dispatch, scheduling and routing functions in medium to large organizations often use sophisticated information technologies like artificial intelligence, robotic process automation, machine learning, and data science models to ensure that raw materials and finished goods inventories are delivered when and where needed. This requires a strong partnership between logistics planning managers, warehouse inventory managers, invoicing and purchase order teams, finance and accounting, and information technology managers. Fortunately, enterprise resource planning tools are available to help facilitate and coordinate these cross-functional collaborations and capabilities.

Information technology managers play a pivotal role in shaping supply chain decisions and analyzing the results of those decisions for retrospectives and forecasts.

In March 2022, the average salary for an IT manager with a supply chain background was $133,500 annually.[49] IT management job postings in

---

[49] Payscale. (2022, March). IT manager, supply chain salary. Retrieved March 6, 2023, from https://www.payscale.com/research/US/Job=IT_Manager%2C_Supply_Chain/Salary

transportation and logistics included:

- Logistics IT Managers

- IT Service Delivery Managers

- Warehousing and Distribution IT Managers

- Director of IT Service Delivery and Operations

- Supply Chain IT Managers

- IT Manager - Enterprise and Architecture

- VP Enterprise Supply Chain

- IT Program Manager - Supply Chain

- Sr. Director IT Business Partner - Manufacturing and Supply Chain

- Manager IT Technology Operations (Systems Engineering Mgr.)

ITM Careers in Entertainment and Sports

Next time you're watching a movie or your favorite TV show, or a music or sports event, consider all the background technologies needed to present it to you, as well as and the data, computers, networks, tablets, smartphones, cabling, satellites, and professionals needed to run it.

As with all modern companies, entertainment production companies require core IT teams to provide information technology services and support to every aspect of their organization. This includes all the standard functions that make an organization viable: accounting and finance, sales, marketing, customer service, human resources, operations, and product development. This provides various career opportunities for software engineers, data scientists, IT architects, database administrators, project managers, business analysis, quality assurance analysts, and many more.

Entertainment production companies consume large volumes of data across various platforms to process video, audio, and social media content. This requires databases designed to process these payloads consistently, reliably, and efficiently. Consider the competing power and IT personnel needed to process applicable gaming theories for sports betting companies or to process the huge loads of audio and video data that streams to radio, television, satellite, and internet platforms. The IT trade professionals required to manage these, and other critical capabilities must acquire and demonstrate an in-depth understanding of these technologies and the workflow processes needed to address them within the entertainment industry.

Many professional and college sports teams employ advanced analytics and data science to improve predictions of success, create simulation models to help minimize and prevent injuries, and even robotic processing automation for specific routine tasks. They hire professionals to develop and deploy these advanced information processing technologies to improve their bottom lines and deliver value-added experiences to their patrons and fans.

One of my personal favorites is ESPN analytics expert Cynthia Frelund, who graduated from Northwestern University with a master of science in predictive analytics. Cynthia is experienced in using tools like Python, R, and Tableau, which are common in data science. She also supports a national nonprofit organization dedicated to the prevention and early detection of ovarian and breast cancer.

IT Management — A Strategic Career Choice

Cynthia has set an excellent example for aspiring young talent motivated to enter the information management sciences and make a difference in moments that matter.

There is a tremendous opportunity in entertainment and sports for information technology professionals with the chance to lead and grow talented technology teams. Managers in this industry carry an exciting challenge to provide stewardship of the overall information ecosystems and collaboratively engineer the Information Management Engine required to wow audiences, entice investors, and produce lifelong fans!

ITM Careers in Information Technology Manufacturing and Services

According to the Bureau of Labor Statistics, the industry with the highest published employment and wages for Computer and Information Systems Managers is "Computer Systems Design and Related Services," which encompasses a broad spectrum of functions and processes from computer infrastructure design, development, sales, marketing, support services, and distribution. This makes sense when you consider that computer manufacturers and service providers require top talent to compete effectively in their markets of choice.

Technology companies need IT trade professionals — specifically developers, engineers, architects, analysts, administrators, and managers — for the same reason every other industry needs them. Computing companies have an extra incentive for attracting, developing, and retaining top management talent because they must demonstrate proficiency in all of these disciplines to have credibility in the eyes of their clients and investors. How can a company sell a customer on a product or service they don't use themselves or on processes and best practices they don't follow?

In May 2021, the industries with the highest levels of employment for computer and information systems managers were:

- Computer systems and design and related services; average annual salary $166, 810

- Software publishers; average annual salary $172,770

- Management, scientific, and technical consulting services; average annual salary $172,220

- Insurance carriers; average annual salary of $162,910

Industries with the highest average annual salaries for computer and information systems managers were:

- Information services, $220,320

- Computer and peripheral equipment manufacturing, $202,530

- Natural gas distribution, $196,840

- Support activities for transportation, $194,680

- Securities, commodity contracts, and other financial investments and related activities, $193,810

The states with the highest annual average salaries for computer and information systems managers were:

- New York, $195,900

- California, $193,500

- New Jersey, $189,540

- Washington, $178,130

- The District of Columbia, $176,000

High-performing information technology managers are vital to many aspects of modern organizations, societies, institutions, and governments. This role is critical because it is directly accountable for delivering the information processing power required to design, engineer, and develop many products and services we depend on to obtain and sustain our chosen standard of living.

Information technology is embedded in so many areas of our lives that it is difficult to itemize them all. And the list of applications and uses of IT is continuously expanding in exciting ways. These innovations require managers and leaders with a desire and commitment to add value to their organization's mission, purpose, objectives, and goals. This requires an essential set of skills, attributes, and aptitudes, including the following:

- Emotional Intelligence

- Problem-Solving

- Analytical Thinking

- Decision-Making

- Written and Oral Communication

- Patience and Empathy

- Technical Aptitude to learn

- Core competency in Technologies of choice

In addition to this list of underlying skills, attributes, and aptitudes, I strongly recommend those interested in IT management to procure a basic understanding of business analysis (i.e., requirements lifecycle management) and project management. IT managers are often accountable for delivering significant outputs to sponsors of their work, such as their direct manager or others in their immediate senior leadership reporting lines.
A fundamental understanding of requirements and project management will go a long way to helping a prospective IT manager plan, coordinate, and collaborate with others to deliver on their expectations. And this basic understanding helps managers with coaching responsibilities, developing, and leading IT business analysts and project managers, in addition to other technical personas on their team.

IT and Related Team Roles and Personas

Computer and information systems teams and closely related disciplines employ an incredible array of roles and personas to deliver value and power to the Information Management Engine. The following list combines the author's 40 years of on-the-job experience and role descriptions from the BLS May 2021 Occupational Employment and Wage Statistics program.

Keep in mind that different organizations often post job descriptions with various degrees of definitions for the following roles, personas, and career opportunities:

IT Analysts

- **Computer Systems Analysts.** Analyze science, engineering, business, and other data processing problems to develop and implement solutions to complex applications problems, system administration issues, or network concerns. Perform systems management and integration functions, improve existing computer systems, and review computer system capabilities, workflow, and schedule limitations. May analyze or recommend commercially available software.

- **Information Security Analysts.** Plan, implement, upgrade, or monitor security measures to protect computer networks and information. Assess system vulnerabilities for security risks and propose and implement risk mitigation strategies. May ensure appropriate security controls are in place to safeguard digital files and vital electronic infrastructure. May respond to computer security breaches and viruses.

- **IT Business Analysts.** Plan, coordinate, and control information technology and supply-side requirements lifecycle activities. This is a critical point to highlight because information technology service providers often have requirements or needs that must be addressed pre-project to enable their capabilities to perform needed services and deliver expected work products. Organizations with heavy data dependencies ignore this at the risk of substantial cost overruns, large amounts of rework, very frustrated IT teams, and highly disgruntled stakeholders.

  IT business analysts also work very closely with business analysts from other functions and departments to ensure the overall information ecosystem is harmonized and balanced to optimize stakeholder value delivery. They help other business analysts translate use-case scenarios and user stories into technical communications. Architects, engineers and developers must ensure alignment and minimize misunderstandings between IT end-users and technology providers.

IT Architects

- **IT Enterprise Architects (EA).** Design and enable the organization's overall architecture of information technology infrastructure capabilities, processes, policies, and standards. Typically, senior-level IT roles in medium to large businesses, EAs are strategists with deep knowledge of current and emerging technologies required to ensure the information technology architecture aligns IT capabilities to support business architecture. They are pivotal in ensuring that IT data models reflect, enable, and support the organization's business models and value drivers.

EAs act as internal consultants to senior executives on significant IT investments and often report directly to the chief information officer or other senior-level executives. Some may also be accountable for planning, coordinating, and harmonizing the activities of solution architects, data architectures, and process architects.
EAs advise and support all levels of the Information Management Engine. I have abiding respect and appreciation for the EAs I've had the distinct pleasure of learning from throughout my career. They tend to be knowledgeable in many areas of the infrastructure, or they can direct a person to the best resource.

- **Solution Architects (SA).** Ensure that information technology infrastructure capabilities deliver the expected outcomes of information requirements management. SAs translate information requirements into existing solutions under a project or program's business case commitments. As the title implies, SAs focus on delivering sustainable solutions to the issues and opportunities their stakeholders encounter.

Data Architects (DA). Design specific data

objects and entities for databases, data lakes, data warehouses, or data factories. A further refinement of the role of solution architect, DAs work closely with data scientists, database administrators, data quality engineers, cybersecurity analysts, and other technical team resources. These collaborations are pivotal to designing and implementing referential integrity between solution applications, databases, and business processes. DAs help to design and document data mappings for extract, transformation and load (ETL) procedures across various data sources into business intelligence and reporting solutions.

- **Computer Network Architects.** Design and implement computer and information networks, such as local area networks (LAN), wide area networks (WAN), intranets, and other forms of data communications networks. Perform network modeling, analysis, and planning, including analysis of capacity needs for network infrastructures. May also design network and computer security measures. May research and recommend network and data communications hardware and software.

IT Developers and Engineers

- **Software Developers and Engineers.** Research, design, and develop computer and network software or specialized utility programs. Analyze user needs and develop software solutions, applying principles and techniques of computer science, engineering, and mathematical analysis. Update software or enhance existing software capabilities. May work with computer hardware engineers to integrate hardware and software systems and develop specifications and performance requirements. May maintain databases within an application area, working individually or coordinating database development as part of a team.

- **Web Developers.** Develop and implement websites, web applications, web application databases, and interactive web interfaces designed to meet particular user experience requirements often documented by business analysts or Agile product owners. They also evaluate their code to ensure it is properly structured, meets industry standards, and is compatible with browsers and devices. Optimize website performance, scalability, and server-side code and processes. May develop website infrastructure and integrate websites with other computer applications.

- **User Experience** (UX) **Developers.** Work closely with website developers, software developers, and solution architects to design digital user interfaces or websites. Develop and test layouts, interfaces, functionality, and navigation menus to ensure compatibility and usability across browsers or devices. May use web framework applications as well as client-side code and processes. May evaluate web design following web and accessibility standards and may analyze web use metrics and optimize websites for marketability and search engine ranking. May design and test interfaces that facilitate human-computer interaction and maximize the usability of digital devices, websites, and software, focusing on aesthetics and design. May create graphics used in websites and manage website content and links.

- **Computer Programmers/Programmer Analysts.** Create, modify, and test the computer code and scripts that allow computer applications to run. Work from requirements, use cases, or user stories drafted by business analysts or Agile product owners. In the case of organizations that follow the waterfall project management methodology, computer programmers may work from technical specifications documents drawn up by business analysts, software and web developers, or others. Programmers may also develop and write computer programs to store, locate, and retrieve specific documents, data, and information.

- **Computer Hardware Engineers.** Research, design, develop, or test computer or computer-related equipment for various uses, including commercial, industrial, military, academic, or scientific use. Some computer hardware engineers may supervise computer or computer-related equipment and components manufacturing and installation.

IT Administrators

- **Database Administrators** (DBAs). Accountable for the organization's databases' availability, security, and stability. Many large to medium-sized companies employ a team of DBAs to ensure all essential databases have a specific owner. DBAs collaborate closely with solution and data architects for database architecture and data model design. Database administrators are directly responsible for database installation, configuration, access security, permission controls, database upgrades and patches, database backup, archival and restoration activities, data loads, log file capture and analysis, database troubleshooting, and ultimately decommissioning at the time of obsolescence.

- **Metadata Catalog Administrators.** Accountable for metadata catalog installation, configuration, upgrades and patches, access security and permission controls, metadata extracts and loads, log file capture and analysis, data catalog troubleshooting, and, ultimately, decommissioning at the time of obsolescence.

  Metadata is data about data; it describes and defines the organization's most critical data elements, metrics, and reports. Metadata catalogs contain the data dictionary (descriptions of specific database tables, columns, types, format, lengths, etc.), business glossary of terms (acronyms, frequently used business words, etc.), critical report, and metrics inventories.

- **Communications Network and Telephony Administrators.** Collaborate closely with computer network architects to install, configure, and maintain an organization's LAN, WAN, data communications network, operating systems, telephone networks, and physical and virtual servers. Perform network and telephony system monitoring and verify the integrity and availability of hardware, network, and server resources and systems.

They analyze network and server resource consumption to ensure the organization has sufficient capacity to process its peak volume loads. These administrators are responsible for network security and collaborate closely with cybersecurity governance teams. Install and upgrade software and maintain software licenses. They may assist in network modeling, analysis, planning, and coordination between network and data communications hardware and software.

IT Service and Support Specialists

- **Computer Network Support Specialists.** Analyze, test, troubleshoot, and evaluate existing network systems, such as LAN, WAN, cloud networks, servers, and other data communications networks. Perform network maintenance to ensure networks operate correctly with minimal interruption within the threshold of service level agreements established with key stakeholders.

  Many commercial organizations rely heavily on network support specialists to maintain business continuity. This is particularly true for cloud computing service companies, social media companies, and any online product or service provider.

- **Computer User Support Specialists** (i.e., help desk). Provide technical assistance to computer users. Answer questions or resolve computer problems for clients in person, via telephone, or electronically. Assist End-users of computer hardware and software, including printing, installation, word processing, electronic mail, and operating systems.

Computer end-user support specialists are often organized into tiers based on their experience and expertise in one or more information and network technologies. First Level support is typically more generalist, and personnel tends to be newer. Second- and third-level support specialists usually have with two or more years of experience, with specialized training in a particular set of technologies to act as a point of escalation when first-level support needs help.

Project and Program Management

- **Project Managers.** Plan, coordinate, communicate, and control an IT project's deliverables within predefined scope, budget, and time constraints. Some project managers are skilled in one or more project management methodologies, including Agile, Scrum, Hybrid, SAFe, PRINCE2, Extreme Programming (XP), Kanban, or traditional Waterfall. Those interested in pursuing competencies in one or more of these methodologies will find several online resources offering classes and certification. Project managers may not report directly to the information technology organization; in large to medium-sized organizations, they may report directly to the project management office or some other function.

- **Scrum Masters.** Lead Scrum Team Sprints, short cycles of software development activities, to deliver specific functionality and features. Sprints usually last from two to four weeks, depending on the complexity of the deliverables. The scrum master is accountable for leading, coordinating, communicating, and controlling the project's expected outcomes.

  Many scrum masters conduct retrospectives after each sprint for continuous performance excellence. They facilitate and harmonize the work of developers, testers, and product owners. Product owners represent the interest of end users and are usually subject-matter-experts in the end-users' workflow processes and use case scenarios.

  Like project managers, Scrum masters may be aligned with other teams or departments besides IT; for example, many report to business intelligence teams outside of IT. They can be found across the organization to represent the core competencies required to manage projects within any function, like finance, accounting, operations, or human resources.

- **Program Managers.** Plan, coordinate, communicate, and control one or more IT projects and project managers within predefined scope, budget, and time constraints. A notable distinction between projects and programs is that projects always have a definite start and end date; programs are typically ongoing and long-term. For instance, a program manager may be accountable for all projects supporting sales and marketing campaigns.

  IT program managers must demonstrate all the

core competencies of IT project managers, plus the ability to lead larger budgets successfully, routinely communicate with senior executives and balance multiple priorities across different sponsoring organizations to deliver measurable program value.

Data Governance

- **Data Governance (DG) Analysts and Managers.** Plan, coordinate, and execute management of data decision rights for governing critical data policies, standards, and controls. These analysts generally report directly to data governance directors or vice presidents. DG analysts must be skilled negotiators, facilitators, and note-takers to help different teams or individuals resolve genuine conflicts and drive compliance. They are risk managers in this way and help to ensure that data management processes and personnel consistently deliver data that is fit for achieving the organization's priorities, goals, and objectives.

- **Data Governance Directors.** Plan, coordinate, communicate, and lead all tasks and activities assigned to data governance managers and analysts. Data governance directors must demonstrate excellent oral and written communication skills to interface with senior executives routinely.

  Interestingly, many organizations align management responsibility for data quality, data literacy, and metadata management with their directors of data governance. This alignment works best when the data governance program is sufficiently sponsored and advocated to the senior levels of the organization. Executive sponsorship and advocacy are vital to the data governance program because data governance is a program that needs to be more understood and one subject to premature failure without consistent, reliable, senior-level sponsorship.

- **Data Stewards.** Represent particular subject matter expertise, experience, and insight about one or more of the organization's data sets, processes, or procedures. This role empowers personnel with a unique responsibility to handle the data assets critical to their teams' success. They usually partner with one or more data quality and governance analysts to ensure these data are fit for intended purposes.

  Data stewards are not usually IT department members; however, some IT teams employ IT data stewards. IT data stewards typically shepherd data internal to the IT function, such as ensuring data processing job logs undergo quality controls or that IT software applications are accurately inventoried, defined, documented, and maintained — any data that the IT functions need for self-reflection and continuous improvement.

Quality Management

- **Data Quality Analysts and Engineers.** Ensure the organization's most critical data meet predefined quality standards and policies. They are accountable for defining the inventory of critical data elements, describing, documenting, and writing data quality control scripts that validate evidence of compliance to predefined acceptance criteria and quality measurement thresholds. This helps to assure data accuracy, completeness, uniqueness, conformity, relevancy, and timeliness to the organization's decision-makers and end-users.

Data quality analysts may report directly to a data quality manager, supervisor, or data governance director. This can vary depending on organizational architecture designs and span of control.

- **Software Quality Assurance Analysts and Testers.** Develop and execute software tests to identify software problems and their causes. Test system modifications to prepare for implementation. Document software and application defects using a bug tracking system and report defects to software or web developers. Create and maintain databases of known defects. Participate in software design reviews to provide input on functional requirements, operational characteristics, product designs, and schedules.

Data Security Management

- **Information Security Analysts.** Plan, implement, upgrade, or monitor security measures to protect computer networks and information. Assess system vulnerabilities for security risks and propose and implement risk mitigation strategies. May ensure appropriate security controls are in place to safeguard digital files and vital electronic infrastructure. May respond to computer security breaches and viruses.

One of their primary responsibilities is to ensure data privacy protections are well-defined and implemented for personally identifiable information (PII).

PII is any data that can be used to discern a person's unique identity by any combination of information, like home address, email address, phone number(s), Social Security number, taxpayer identification, bank account number, or any other data element traceable to a particular person. This also includes personal health information (PHI) in the medical and pharmaceutical industries. PHI includes essential pieces of data in a person's medical records. This not only prevents the identification of a person but also helps to prevent discrimination based on medical conditions.

Business Intelligence and Analytics

- **Business Intelligence (BI) Analysts.** Responsible for the digital transformation, visualization, and reporting of raw data into insightful business intelligence and operational reports needed to solve problems, answer questions, make decisions, and turn opportunities into valuable results. BI analysts develop, analyze and communicate informative narratives that tell compelling stories to intended audiences.

  They often collaborate closely with data scientists, statistical analysts, and research and development professionals. Collectively they explore targeted insights into market opportunities and risks, potential industry disruptions, competitive product introductions, vendor performance, customer sentiments and behaviors, and product and service quality. This group of professionals may or may not reside directly in the IT department; sometimes, they align to shared services and finance or are spread across sales, marketing, and operations teams.

- **Data Scientists.** Employ a combination of data management expertise, math, and statistics to develop and analyze models. These models help explain and predict specific customer behavior patterns, vendor performance, or competitor reactions. They are instrumental in diagnosing particular root causes and helping answer essential questions. Data scientists are crucial to accurately understanding the organization's real value drivers and the primary causes of expected outcomes.

  Data science is the study and application of data analytics to drive diagnostic (what happened and why), predictive (what will happen and when), and prescriptive (how do we fix it and prevent it) investigation of an organization's internal and external environments, and processes of decision making and problem-solving.

- **Computer and Information Research Scientists.** Conduct research into fundamental computer and information science as theorists, designers, or inventors. Develop solutions to problems in the field of computer hardware and software.

- **Statisticians.** Develop or apply mathematical or statistical theory and methods to collect, organize, interpret, and summarize numerical

data to provide usable information. May
specialize in biostatistics, informatics,
agriculture, business, economics, or any field
of informatics. Includes mathematical and
survey statisticians.

- **Statistical Assistants.** Compile and compute
  data according to statistical formulas for use
  in statistical studies. May perform actuarial
  computations and compile charts and graphs for
  use by actuaries.

PART V: Celebrate Diversity of Thought, Inclusion & Performance Excellence

Information technology is a growing industry with a high demand for skilled professionals, yet it has been historically dominated by a fairly narrow demographic, perspective, and cultural background. However, a consistent push has been made to increase the diversity of thought and experiences in the field and create more opportunities for women and minorities.

Diversity of thought refers to the idea that diverse backgrounds, experiences, and perspectives can lead to better organizational decision-making and problem-solving. This concept emphasizes that diversity in race, gender, age, and other dimensions is essential, but the diversity of thought is equally important. Diversity of thought enables a variety of perspectives to be brought to the table, leading to more creativity, innovation, and effectiveness. It also helps organizations avoid groupthink and make better decisions.[50]

Diversity in thought is good for the bottom line, too. A 2013 Harvard Business Review article on diversity of thought described *two-dimensional diversity:* leaders who exhibit at least three inherent traits (such as gender, sexual orientation, and ethnicity) alongside at least three traits acquired through experience. The researchers found that employees of firms with two-dimensional

---

[50] Richard, O. C., McMillan-Capehart, A., & Burnett, M. F. (2019). Diversity of thought and its impact on group creativity and innovation. *Journal of Applied Behavioral Science, 55*(2), 137-153. doi: 10.1177/0021886318822596.

diversity were 45% more likely to report a growth in market share over the previous year and 70% more likely to report that the company captured a new market.[51]

In this section, we will examine the current state of women and minorities in IT careers, their challenges, and the factors contributing to their success.

The Current State of Women and Minorities in IT Careers –

The current state of women and minorities in IT careers can be analyzed by looking at representation, pay, and job opportunities.

- **Representation.** Women and minorities are significantly underrepresented in IT careers. According to a National Center for Women & Information Technology report, women make up only 26% of the computing workforce. African Americans and Hispanics comprise only 9% and 7%, respectively.[52]
- **Pay.** The gender pay gap is also prevalent in IT careers. According to a study by Hired, women in tech make 3% less than men on average. This gap is even more significant for women of color, with Black women making 7% less and Hispanic women making 12% less than their male counterparts.[53]

---

[51] Hewlett, Sylvia Ann, Melinda Marshall, and Laura Sherbin. "How Diversity Can Drive Innovation." Harvard Business Review, December 2013, Retrieved from https://hbr.org/2013/12/how-diversity-can-drive-innovation.

[52] National Center for Women & Information Technology. (2021). By the numbers. Retrieved from https://www.ncwit.org/resources/by-the-numbers.

[53] Hired. (2019). The State of Wage Inequality in the Workplace. Retrieved from https://hired.com/state-of-wage-inequality-in-the-workplace

- **Job Opportunities.** Women and minorities also face challenges in obtaining job opportunities in the IT field. A National Bureau of Economic Research study found that applicants with "white-sounding" names were 36% more likely to receive a call back for an interview than those with "African American-sounding" names, even with identical resumes.[54]

Challenges Faced by Women and Minorities in IT Careers

Women and minorities face challenges in IT careers, including a lack of representation and mentorship, a hostile work environment, and discrimination.

- **Lack of Representation and Mentorship.** A lack of representation and mentorship can make it challenging for women and minorities to break into the field and advance in their careers. Finding role models and mentors who share similar experiences and can provide guidance and support can be difficult.
- **Hostile Work Environment.** Women and minorities also face a hostile work environment, with a high incidence of sexism and racism. According to a survey by the Kapor Center, 37% of Black and Latina women in tech reported experiencing gender bias; 17% of white women said they had experienced gender bias.[55],[56]

---

[54] Bertrand, M., & Mullainathan, S. (2004). Are Emily and Brendan More Employable than Lakisha and Jamal? A Field Experiment on Labor Market Discrimination. *The American Economic Review, 94*(4), 991-1013. doi: 10.1257/0002828042002561

[55] Chou, R. S., & Feagin, J. R. (2015). The myth of the post-racial era: The continuing significance of race in the United States. Routledge.

[56] Kapor Center. (2017). Tech Leavers Study. Retrieved from https://www.kaporcenter.org/tech-leavers/

- **Discrimination.** Discrimination can also manifest in subtle ways, such as microaggressions, which can have a cumulative effect on an individual's well-being and career advancement. A study in the Harvard Business Review found that microaggressions have a more significant impact on women and minorities than overt discrimination.[57]

Factors that Contribute to the Success of Women and Minorities in IT Careers

Despite the challenges faced by women and minorities in IT careers, several factors contribute to their success.

- **Education.** Education is a crucial factor in the success of women and minorities in IT careers. Studies have found that women and minorities who have a degree in a STEM field are more likely to enter and advance in the IT field.[58],[59]

- **Mentorship.** Mentorship is also an essential factor in the success of women and minorities in IT careers. Studies have found that having a

---

[57] Sue, D. W., Capodilupo, C. M., Torino, G. C., Bucceri, J. M., Holder, A. M. B., Nadal, K. L., & Esquilin, M. (2007). Racial microaggressions in everyday life: Implications for clinical practice. *American Psychologist, 62*(4), 271-286. doi: 10.1037/0003-066X.62.4.271.

[58] National Science Foundation. (2019). Women, Minorities, and Persons with Disabilities in Science and Engineering: 2019. Retrieved from https://ncses.nsf.gov/pubs/nsf19304/digest/about-this-report

[59] National Center for Women & Information Technology. (2016). By the Numbers: Women in Tech. Retrieved from https://www.ncwit.org/resources/by-the-numbers-women-in-tech.

mentor can increase job satisfaction, job performance, and career advancement.[60],[61]

- **Networking.** Networking is another critical factor in the success of women and minorities in IT careers. Studies have found that women and minorities who participate in professional organizations and attend networking events are more likely to advance in their careers.[62],[63]

Best Practices for Increasing the Success of Women and Minorities in IT Careers

Several best practices can be implemented to increase the success of women and minorities in IT careers.

- **Diversity and Inclusion Initiatives.** Diversity and inclusion initiatives can be implemented to increase the representation of women and minorities in IT careers. These initiatives may include unconscious bias training for hiring managers and recruiters, targeted recruitment efforts to reach underrepresented groups, and creating a diverse and inclusive workplace culture.

- **Mentorship and Sponsorship Programs.** Mentorship and sponsorship programs can be established to provide guidance and support for women and

[60] Johnson, W. B., & Smith, M. B. (2018). A review of mentorship in academic medicine. *American Journal of Medicine, 131*(3), 251-256. doi: 10.1016/j.amjmed.2017.10.037.

[61] Kim, E., & Kim, T. (2019). The effects of mentorship on job satisfaction and career success among South Korean IT professionals. *Journal of Information Technology Management, 30*(3), 30-41.

[62] Brown-Glaude, W. (2010). Networking as a professional development tool for women and minorities. *New Directions for Student Services, 2010*(131), 59-68. doi: 10.1002/ss.376

[63] National Center for Women & Information Technology. (2016). Women in Tech: The Facts. Retrieved from https://www.ncwit.org/resources/women-tech-facts.

minorities in IT careers. These programs can pair women and minority professionals with mentors and sponsors who can provide career advice, networking opportunities, and help with navigating the workplace.

- **Employee Resource Groups.** Employee resource groups (ERGs) can be established to provide a sense of community and support for women and minorities in IT careers. ERGs can offer networking opportunities, professional development opportunities, and a platform for advocating for diversity and inclusion within the company.

- **Flexible Work Arrangements.** Flexible work arrangements, such as remote work and flexible schedules, can help women and minorities balance work and family responsibilities. These arrangements can also help to reduce the impact of microaggressions and other forms of discrimination by allowing individuals to work in environments that are more supportive and inclusive.

A Case Summary: Promoting Equity and Innovation in the U.S. R&D Information Ecosystem

The U.S. research and development information ecosystem is a complex and dynamic network of government agencies, academic institutions, private companies, and international partners that work together to advance scientific knowledge, develop new technologies, and drive economic growth and innovation.[64] While the ecosystem has many strengths, it also faces significant equity, diversity, and transparency challenges.

One challenge facing this ecosystem is the need to promote equity and diversity in STEM fields. Women and minorities remain underrepresented in STEM occupations, particularly in information technology.[65] According to the National Center for Women & Information Technology, women hold only 25% of computing occupations, and minorities hold only 16% of these occupations.[66]

Another challenge is the need to address data privacy and security concerns. With the proliferation of digital technologies and the increasing use of big data, there is a growing concern about how personal data is being collected, stored, and used.[67] Data security and privacy are essential for maintaining public trust and promoting innovation in the

---

[64] National Science Board. (2018). Science & Engineering Indicators 2018. Retrieved from https://www.nsf.gov/statistics/2018/nsb20181/report/sections/highlights
[65] Bureau of Labor Statistics. (2021). Computer and Information Technology Occupations. Retrieved from https://www.bls.gov/ooh/computer-and-information-technology/home.htm
[66] National Center for Women & Information Technology. (2021). By the Numbers. Retrieved from https://www.ncwit.org/infographic/by-the-numbers
[67] Pew Research Center. (2021). Internet/Broadband Fact Sheet. Retrieved from https://www.pewresearch.org/internet/fact-sheet/internet-broadband/

ecosystem.

Fostering open and transparent scientific practices is another challenge facing the U.S. R&D information ecosystem. Open science, which involves sharing research data, methods, and findings with the scientific community and the public, can accelerate scientific progress and increase the impact of research.[68] However, there are concerns about the potential misuse of open data and the need to ensure that data is properly curated and maintained.

Efforts are underway to address these challenges in the U.S. R&D information ecosystem. For example, the National Institutes of Health's National Center for Advancing Translational Sciences (NCATS) is working to promote diversity and inclusion in translational science, which involves the application of scientific discoveries to improve health outcomes.[69] The National Science Foundation's INCLUDES program is also working to increase diversity and inclusion in STEM fields.[70]

The National Institutes of Health's data-sharing policy requires that data from NIH-funded research be shared with the scientific community, and the agency has developed an open science policy to promote transparency and collaboration.[71],[72] The development of open science infrastructure, such as data

---

[68] Microsoft. (2020). The Future Computed: AI and its role in society. Retrieved from https://www.microsoft.com/en-us/ai/future-computed

[69] National Institutes of Health. (2021). National Center for Advancing Translational Sciences. Retrieved from https://ncats.nih.gov/

[70] National Science Foundation. (2021). INCLUDES: Inclusion across the Nation of Communities of Learners of Underrepresented Discoverers in Engineering and Science. Retrieved from https://www.nsf.gov/funding/pgm_summ.jsp?pims_id=505289

[71] National Institutes of Health. (2021). Data Sharing Policy. Retrieved from https://osp.od.nih.gov/scientific-sharing/policy/

[72] National Institutes of Health. (2021). Open Science. Retrieved from https://www.nih.gov/research-training/open-science

repositories and collaborative research platforms, is also helping to promote open and transparent scientific practices.

International collaboration is another important aspect of the U.S. R&D information ecosystem. Collaboration with researchers from different countries and regions can bring new perspectives, expertise, and resources to scientific projects, leading to breakthroughs and discoveries that would not have been possible otherwise.[73]

Overall, promoting equity, diversity, and innovation in the U.S. R&D information ecosystem is critical for advancing scientific progress and improving people's lives. By investing in STEM education and training, promoting diversity and inclusion, addressing data privacy and security concerns, fostering open and transparent scientific practices, and engaging in international collaboration, we can ensure that the ecosystem remains open, transparent, and equitable for all participants.

In conclusion, the success of women and minorities in IT careers is essential for creating a diverse and inclusive workforce. While there are many challenges that women and minorities face in the field, many factors also contribute to their success. Companies can create a more inclusive and supportive workplace culture that benefits all employees by implementing best practices, such as diversity and inclusion initiatives, mentorship and sponsorship programs, and flexible work arrangements.

---

[73] National Academies of Sciences, Engineering, and Medicine. (2018). The Impact of International Scientific Collaboration on the U.S. Research Enterprise. Retrieved from https://www.nap.edu/catalog/25114/the-impact-of-international-scientific-collaboration-on-the-us-research-enterprise

The Information Management Engine

Conclusion

The primal need for accurate, timely, and relevant information has driven living organisms' survival and growth for hundreds of millions of years. Information is an essential survival requirement for all living organisms, including organizations formed by them.

As IT professionals, we must maintain sight of the critical nature of information in every aspect of the operation, especially when it involves the passionate expression of primary stakeholders' personal values and motivations. The primary purpose of this book is to enable organizations to deliver stakeholder value through a practice model of essential information management trade-practices, in concert with other business management disciplines.

The combination of emotional and objective motivation for better information is a potent stimulus and critical ingredient of actionable insight concerning which internal and external factors are most urgent and relevant for a person, team, or organization to prioritize. Information has been and is a significant success factor in the lifecycles of all living organisms. It is as vital to life and organization as water is to rain and sunlight to sunrise. therefore, it is imperative to manage the information technologies we use to reap the inherent benefits of valuable information in every economic condition.

Managing information technologies such as computers, smartphones, microchips, telecommunications equipment, and related technologies is essential in achieving predictable investor returns and customer-perceived value outcomes. Increasing returns, growing profit margins, decreasing operating costs, and improving customer experiences are the primary motives for commercial investment. It is also important to acknowledge that people are inundated with overwhelming volumes of data; IT professionals must manage it effectively to harness its potential benefits.

The content of this book is an essential resource for business owners, organization leaders, computer users, and knowledge workers looking to harness the potential of their data assets and information technologies to achieve high-priority objectives and value metrics. The Information Management Engine value-delivery model of keystone information management trade-practices provides a simple, comprehensive approach to managing information effectively, enabling organizations to deliver stakeholder value and meet the undeniable challenges of the Business Ultimatum.

About The Author

Gerrold Kimbrough is a skilled Information Management professional passionate about the role of data and information in many aspects of Life in the Digital Age.

He has over 40 years of hands-on experience in large, complex organizations in Leadership, Coaching & Training, Technical Development, Process & Project Management, Business Analysis, Master Data Governance, and Data Quality Management.

His hobbies include reading books and listening to the music of many different genres, writing song lyrics, poems, and books, hiking, biking, and many forms of sports entertainment.

References

1. Wiles, J. (2018). Employees Seek Personal Value and Purpose at Work. Be Prepared to Deliver. Gartner. Retrieved from https://www.gartner.com/smarterwithgartner/employees-seek-personal-value-and-purpose-at-work-be-prepared-to-deliver/
2. Eisenberger, R., Stinglhamber, F., Vandenberghe, C., Sucharski, I. L., & Rhoades, L. (2002). Perceived supervisor support: Contributions to perceived organizational support and employee retention. Journal of applied psychology, 87(3), 565.
3. Salovey, P., & Mayer, J. D. (1990). Emotional intelligence. Imagination, cognition and personality, 9(3), 185-211. doi: 10.2190/DUGG-P24E-52WK-6CDG
4. Goleman, D. (1995). Emotional Intelligence: Why It Can Matter More Than IQ. Bantam Books.
5. Bradberry, T., & Greaves, J. (2009). Emotional intelligence 2.0. TalentSmart.
6. National Science Foundation. (n.d.). Cosmic Microwave Background Radiation. Retrieved from https://www.nsf.gov/news/special_reports/cosmicmicrowave/
7. Cameron, K. S., & Quinn, R. E. (2011). Diagnosing and changing organizational culture: Based on the competing values framework. John Wiley & Sons.
8. Huang, L., & Hsu, C. W. (2016). The impact of organizational culture on the relationship

between shared leadership and team creativity. International Journal of Human Resource Management, 27(8), 854-871.

9. Walton, M. (1989). The Deming Management Method. New York, NY: Perigee Books.

10. Loshin, D. (2010). Master Data Management. Elsevier Inc. p. 82.

11. Data Management Association. (2009). Data Management Body of Knowledge (2nd ed.). Technics Publications.

12. Skills Framework for the Information Age (SFIA-Online.org). (n.d.). Solution Architecture. Retrieved from https://www.sfia-online.org/en/framework/sfia-7/skills/solution-architecture

13. The Open Group - https://www.opengroup.org/.

14. ITIL 4 Foundation, Axelos, 2019, Chapter 2. The website for Axelos ITIL 4 is https://www.axelos.com/best-practice-solutions/itil.

15. ITIL 4 Foundation, Axelos, 2019, Chapter 3.

16. McLeod, R., & Schell, G. (2019). Management Information Systems (pp. 45-68). Pearson.

17. Laudon, K. C., & Laudon, J. P. (2018). Management Information Systems: Managing the Digital Firm (pp. 91-112). Pearson.

18. McLeod, R., & Schell, G. (2019), pp. 69-92.

19. Laudon, K. C., & Laudon, J. P. (2018), pp. 345-358.

20. McLeod, R., & Schell, G. (2019), pp. 93-114.

21. Laudon, K. C., & Laudon, J. P. (2018) pp. 610-625.

22. McLeod, R., & Schell, G. (2019), pp. 115-132.

23. Harter, J. K., Schmidt, F. L., & Hayes, T. L. (2002). Business-unit-level relationship between employee satisfaction, employee engagement, and business outcomes: A meta-analysis. Journal of Applied Psychology, 87(2), 268-279. doi: 10.1037//0021-9010.87.2.268

24. Young, S. D., & O'Byrne, S. F. (2001). EVA and Value-Based Management: A Practical Guide to Implementation. McGraw-Hill Professional.

25. Stewart, B. (1991). Economic Value Added (EVA) - The Real Key to Creating Wealth. New York: Simon & Schuster, p. 173.

26. Appraisal Institute. (2019). The Appraisal of Real Estate (15th ed.). Chicago, IL: Appraisal Institute. Retrieved from https://www.appraisalinstitute.org/the-appraisal-of-real-estate-15th-edition/

27. Data Management Association International. (2017). Data Management Body of Knowledge (2nd ed.). Tampa, FL: Technics Publications. P. 354.

28. Cambridge Dictionary, s.v. "Stakeholder," accessed March 6, 2023, https://dictionary.cambridge.org/dictionary/english/stakeholder.

29. Merriam-Webster. (n.d.). Emotive. In Merriam-Webster.com Dictionary. Retrieved March 29, 2022, from https://www.merriam-webster.com/dictionary/emotive.

30. Kaplan, R. S., & Norton, D. P. (1992). The balanced scorecard--Measures that drive performance. Harvard Business Review, 70(1), 71-79.

31.   Koch, C. (2003). The real business value of IT. CIO Magazine. Retrieved from https://www.cio.com/article/2441977/the-real-business-value-of-it.html

32.   White, S. K. (2018, September 4). What is OKR? A goal-setting framework for thinking. CIO Magazine. Retrieved from https://www.cio.com/article/3213590/what-is-okr-a-goal-setting-framework-for-thinking-big.html

33.   Hurd, M., & Nyberg, B. (2004). The value factor: How global leaders use information for growth and competitive advantage. New York, NY: McGraw-Hill.pg. 62,63

34.   Porter, M. E. (1980). Competitive strategy: Techniques for analyzing industries and competitors. New York, NY: The Free Press.

35.   Carkenord, B. A. (2009). Seven steps to mastering business analysis (p. 126). Fort Lauderdale, FL: J. Ross Publishing.

36.   U.S. Bureau of Labor Statistics. (n.d.). Computer and information systems managers. Retrieved March 6, 2023, from https://www.bls.gov/ooh/management/computer-and-information-systems-managers.htm

37.   ZipRecruiter. (2023, January 15). Top ten highest paying cities for educational technology jobs. Retrieved March 6, 2023, from https://www.ziprecruiter.com/blog/10-highest-paying-cities-for-educational-technology-jobs/

38.   American Medical Informatics Association. (n.d.). AMIA certification program. Retrieved March 6, 2023, from https://www.amia.org/certification

39.   Comparably. (2022). HR technology manager salary. Retrieved March 6, 2023, from

https://www.comparably.com/salaries/salaries-for-hr-technology-manager

40. Glassdoor. (2023, January). IT finance manager salary. Retrieved March 6, 2023, from https://www.glassdoor.com/Salaries/it-finance-manager-salary-SRCH_KO0,18.htm

41. Payscale. (2022, March). IT manager, supply chain salary. Retrieved March 6, 2023, from https://www.payscale.com/research/US/Job=IT_Manager%2C_Supply_Chain/Salary

42. Richard, O. C., McMillan-Capehart, A., & Burnett, M. F. (2019). Diversity of thought and its impact on group creativity and innovation. Journal of Applied Behavioral Science, 55(2), 137-153. doi: 10.1177/0021886318822596.

43. Hewlett, Sylvia Ann, Melinda Marshall, and Laura Sherbin. "How Diversity Can Drive Innovation." Harvard Business Review, December 2013, Retrieved from https://hbr.org/2013/12/how-diversity-can-drive-innovation.

44. National Center for Women & Information Technology. (2021). By the numbers. Retrieved from https://www.ncwit.org/resources/by-the-numbers.

45. Hired. (2019). The State of Wage Inequality in the Workplace. Retrieved from https://hired.com/state-of-wage-inequality-in-the-workplace

46. Bertrand, M., & Mullainathan, S. (2004). Are Emily and Brendan More Employable than Lakisha and Jamal? A Field Experiment on Labor Market Discrimination. The American Economic Review, 94(4), 991-1013. doi: 10.1257/0002828042002561

47.   Chou, R. S., & Feagin, J. R. (2015). The myth of the post-racial era: The continuing significance of race in the United States. Routledge.

48.   Kapor Center. (2017). Tech Leavers Study. Retrieved from https://www.kaporcenter.org/tech-leavers/

49.   Sue, D. W., Capodilupo, C. M., Torino, G. C., Bucceri, J. M., Holder, A. M. B., Nadal, K. L., & Esquilin, M. (2007). Racial microaggressions in everyday life: Implications for clinical practice. American Psychologist, 62(4), 271-286. doi: 10.1037/0003-066X.62.4.271.

50.   National Science Foundation. (2019). Women, Minorities, and Persons with Disabilities in Science and Engineering: 2019. Retrieved from https://ncses.nsf.gov/pubs/nsf19304/digest/about-this-report

51.   National Center for Women & Information Technology. (2016). By the Numbers: Women in Tech. Retrieved from https://www.ncwit.org/resources/by-the-numbers-women-in-tech.

52.   Johnson, W. B., & Smith, M. B. (2018). A review of mentorship in academic medicine. American Journal of Medicine, 131(3), 251-256. doi: 10.1016/j.amjmed.2017.10.037.

53.   Kim, E., & Kim, T. (2019). The effects of mentorship on job satisfaction and career success among South Korean IT professionals. Journal of Information Technology Management, 30(3), 30-41.

54.   Brown-Glaude, W. (2010). Networking as a professional development tool for women and minorities. New Directions for Student

Services, 2010(131), 59-68. doi:
10.1002/ss.376
55.   National Center for Women & Information
Technology. (2016). Women in Tech: The Facts.
Retrieved from
https://www.ncwit.org/resources/women-tech-
facts.
56.   National Science Board. (2018). Science &
Engineering Indicators 2018. Retrieved from
https://www.nsf.gov/statistics/2018/nsb20181/
report/sections/highlights
57.   Bureau of Labor Statistics. (2021).
Computer and Information Technology
Occupations. Retrieved from
https://www.bls.gov/ooh/computer-and-
information-technology/home.htm
58.   National Center for Women & Information
Technology. (2021). By the Numbers. Retrieved
from https://www.ncwit.org/infographic/by-
the-numbers
59.   Pew Research Center. (2021).
Internet/Broadband Fact Sheet. Retrieved from
https://www.pewresearch.org/internet/fact-
sheet/internet-broadband/
60.   Microsoft. (2020). The Future Computed:
AI and its role in society. Retrieved from
https://www.microsoft.com/en-us/ai/future-
computed
61.   National Institutes of Health. (2021).
National Center for Advancing Translational
Sciences. Retrieved from
https://ncats.nih.gov/
62.   National Science Foundation. (2021).
INCLUDES: Inclusion across the Nation of
Communities of Learners of Underrepresented
Discoverers in Engineering and Science.
Retrieved from

https://www.nsf.gov/funding/pgm_summ.jsp?pims_id=505289

63.   National Institutes of Health. (2021). Data Sharing Policy. Retrieved from https://osp.od.nih.gov/scientific-sharing/policy/

64.   National Institutes of Health. (2021). Open Science. Retrieved from https://www.nih.gov/research-training/open-science

65.   National Academies of Sciences, Engineering, and Medicine. (2018). The Impact of International Scientific Collaboration on the U.S. Research Enterprise. Retrieved from https://www.nap.edu/catalog/25114/the-impact-of-international-scientific-collaboration-on-the-us-research-enterprise

Bibliography

Autrey, J. A. (1991). *Love & Profit : The Art of Caring Leadership.* New York: William Morrow and Company, Inc.

Blanchard, K., Robinson, D., & Robinson, J. (1995). *Zap the Gaps!* (1st ed.). New York: Harper Collins.

Brynjolfsson, E., & Hit, L. M. (n.d.).

Carkenord, B. A. (2009). *Seven Steps to Mastering Business Analysis* (1st ed.). Lord Lauderdale: J. Ross Publishing, Inc.

Cassidy, A., & Cassidy, D. (2010). *A Practical guide to Reducing IT Costs* (1st ed.). Lauderdale and, FL, United States: J. Ross Publishing, Inc.

Covey, S. R. (1989). *The Seven Habits of Highly Effective People* (1st ed.). New York, New York: Simon and Schuster.

Covey, S. R. (1990). *Principle-Centered Leadership* (1st ed.). New York: Summit Books.

Davenport, T., Harris, J., & Morison, R. (2010). *Analytics at Work.* Boston: Harvard Business School Publishing Corporation.

Debevoise, N. T. (1999). *The Data Warehouse Method.* Upper Saddle River: Prentice-Hall.

Eureka, W. E., & Ryan, N. E. (1988). *The Customer-Driven Company.* Dearborn, Michigan, United States: ASI Press.

Fadem, T. J. (2009). *The Art Of Asking.* Upper Saddle River, New Jersey, United States: Pearson Education, Inc. Publishing as, FT Press.

BIBLIOGRAPHY

Fewster, M., & Graham, D. (1999). *Software Test Automation* (1st ed.). Harlow, England: Addison-Wesley.

Freese, T. A. (2003). *Secrets of Question Based Selling*. Naperville, Illinois, United States: Sourcebooks, Inc.

Gates, B. (1999). *Business @ The Speed of Thought* (1st ed.). New York, New York, United States: Warner Books, Inc.

Gaynor, G. H. (2002). *Innovation by Design* (1st ed.). New York: AMACOM, a division of American Management Association.

Hill, N. (1991). *The Law of Success* (49th ed.). Evanston: Success Unlimited, PMA Communications, Inc.

Hubbard, D. W. (2014). *How To Measure Anything* (3rd ed.). Hoboken, New Jersey: John Wiley & Sons, Inc.

Hurd, M., & Nyberg, L. (2004). *The Value factor* (1st ed.). Princeton, New Jersey: Bloomberg Press.

International Institute of Business Analysis. (2009). *A Guide to the Business Analysis Body of Knowledge* (Version 2.0 ed.). Ontario: International Institute of Business Analysis.

Kadlec, J. (2004). *The Rational Guide to IT Project Management*. (G. Robidoux, Ed.) Greenland, New Hampshire: Rational Press-, an imprint of the Mann Publishing Group.

Kaydos, W. (1991). *Measuring, Managing and Maximizing Performance* (1st ed.). Cambridge, MA: Productivity Press, Inc.

Kempis, R.-D., & Ringbeck, J. (1999). *Do IT Smart* (1st ed.). New York: The Free Press, a division of Simon & Schuster, Inc.

Marakas, G. M. (1999). *Decision-Support Systems in the 21st Century* (1st ed.). (P. J. Boardman, Ed.) Upper Saddle River: Prentice-Hall.

McGuff, F., & Kador, J. (1999). *Developing Analytical Database Applications* (1st ed.). (K. M. Karen, Ed.) Upper Saddle River: Prentice-Hall.

Meltzer, M. F. (1981). *Information The Ultimate Management Resource* (1st ed.). New York: AMACOM, a Division of American Management Association.

Murch, R. (2001). *Project Management Best Practices for IT Professionals*. Up, Saddle River, New Jersey, United States: Prentice-Hall, Inc.

Nadler, D. A., Gerstein, M., Shaw, R., & And, A. (1992). *Organizational Architecture: Designs for Changing Organizations*. San Francisco, California, United States: Jossey-Bass.

National Research Council of National Academies. (2009). *Assessing the Impacts of Changes in the Information Technology R&D Ecosystem: Retaining Leadership in an Increasingly Global Environment*. National Academy of Sciences. Washington, DC: National Academies Press. Retrieved from http://www.nap.edu/catalog/12174/assessing-the-impacts-of-changes-in-the-information-technology-rd-ecosystem

Nickerson, R. C. (2000). *Business and Information Systems* (2nd ed.). (M. Cox, Ed.) Upper Saddle River: Prentice-Hall.

BIBLIOGRAPHY

Nirenberg, J. (1993). *The Living Organization*. New York, New York: Irwin and Professional Publishing.

Project Management Institute. (2004). *A Guide to the Project Management Body of Knowledge* (3rd ed.). (P. Publishing, Ed.) Newtown Square, PA, United States: PMI Publishing.

Western Electric Company Inc. (1985). *Statistical Quality Control Handbook* (11th Printing ed.). Charlotte: Delmar Printing Company.

www.ingramcontent.com/pod-product-compliance
Lightning Source LLC
Chambersburg PA
CBHW061140220326
41599CB00025B/4301